BANKERS as BROKERS

The Complete Guide to Selling Mutual Funds, Annuities and Other Fee-Based Investment Products

Merlin Gackle
with the Senior Managers of
INVEST Financial Corporation
and Bob Andelman

Project Editor, Allan Priaulx

A BANKLINE PUBLICATION
PROBUS PUBLISHING COMPANY
Chicago, Illinois
Cambridge, England

A BankLine Publication

© 1994, Probus Publishing Company

ALL RIGHTS RESERVED. No part of this publication may be reproduced, stored in a retrieval system, or transmitted, in any form or by any means, electronic, mechanical, photocopying, recording, or otherwise, without the prior written permission of the publisher and the author.

This publication is designed to provide accurate and authoritative information in regard to the subject matter covered. It is sold with the understanding that the author and the publisher are not engaged in rendering legal, accounting, or other professional service.

Authorization to photocopy items for internal or personal use, or the internal or personal use of specific clients, is granted by PROBUS PUBLISHING COMPANY, provided that the U.S. $7.00 per page fee is paid directly to Copyright Clearance Center, 222 Rosewood Drive, Danvers, MA 01923, USA; Phone: 1-508-750-8400. For those organizations that have been granted a photocopy license by CCC, a separate system of payment has been arranged. The fee code for users of the Transactional Reporting Service is 1-55738-702-8/94/$00.00 + $7.00.

ISBN 1-55738-702-8

Printed in the United States of America

BB

1 2 3 4 5 6 7 8 9 0

BH

> Probus books are available at quantity discounts when purchased for business, educational, or sales promotional use. For more information, please call the Director, Corporate / Institutional Sales at (800) 998-4644, or write:
>
> Director, Corporate / Institutional Sales
> Probus Publishing Company
> 1925 N. Clybourn Avenue
> Chicago, IL 60614
> PHONE (800) 998-4644   FAX (312) 868-6250

For the men and women of *INVEST*,
who make each day count.

Table of Contents

Acknowledgments vii

Introduction ix

1. Bankers as Brokers:
   The Reality of the Business 1
2. Building a Better Bank through Brokerage . . 17
3. Due Diligence for Today and Tomorrow:
   Looking at the Products 43
4. The Marketing Secrets 59
5. Everyone Back to School 83
6. Financial Planning—
   Leveraging Customer Trust 97
7. Integration of the Investment Program . . . 115
8. Brokerage in Community Banks 129
9. Compliance 139
10. The Future of Investment
    Products and Banking 155

Appendixes:

A. Glossary of Terms 173

B. A Third-Party Marketing Audit 193

About the Authors 199

Index 213

Acknowledgments

Bringing together the experiences of a national organization as diverse as *INVEST* Financial Corporation requires the cooperation, contributions, and support of a vast network of executives, managers, and staffers. Appreciation is conveyed to everyone whose individual contributions make this book possible.

The authors would especially like to acknowledge the input and ideas offered by *INVEST's* Chairman, Don Eller, and its senior management team: Bob Burke, Mary Ann Goodrum, Joel Kesner, Ellen McCorkle, Lou Newtson, John Richter, Lynn Smelt, Jeff Thornton, and Ted Wdowiak. The entire *INVEST* staff provided information, either directly or indirectly, which formed the basis for this book; special thanks go to John Bertino, Ann Cody, Jeannie Holliday, and Calvin Nystrom. Betty Carlin was especially invaluable in coordinating this book and keeping the authors on track.

Also participating in the information gathering process were Phil Broyles (Top Producer), Lyle Sorum (Bremer Financial Services), Ken Hughes (Cal Fed Investment Services), and Tom Miers (MidAmerica Federal Savings Bank).

Particular thanks are extended to Stephen Burke and Jim Neiland (Dreyfus Service Corp.), Dean Kopperud and Lee Rosenblum (Fortis Financial Group), David Minella and Ray Cunningham (G.T. Global), John Peters (Kemper Financial Services), Brad Powell (Keyport Life Insurance), William Shiebler (Putnam Financial Services), and Scott West and Ann Marie Klingenhagen (Van Kampen Merritt) whose invaluable input and insight about the industry made this project possible.

And finally, we would like to express deep appreciation to Allan Priaulx (Resource Media Inc.) for the months of work he dedicated to developing this book from an initial idea to reality and whose help in directing us through every step, supplying ideas for additional topics and reworking initial drafts to final form was the key to this book's successful completion.

Introduction

The banking world is participating in a dramatic change in the way people acquire, own, hold, and distribute financial products and plan their lives from a financial standpoint. The transformation is occurring at a dizzying pace.

Our goal in *Bankers as Brokers* is two-fold: first, to show how alternative products can help bankers bring a new focus on the basics of their business; second, to peek into the future, a tomorrow at once disturbing and foreign, yet as promising as anything the banking and investment industries ever knew in the past.

The common concerns of most bankers today center around four essential areas: controlling expenses, identifying profitable niches for serving customer needs, providing superior customer service, and adhering to sound credit underwriting. Bank participation in the investment products business will have a dramatic impact on the first three concerns in both traditional and newer areas of the bank.

Banks are driving a fundamental shift in the distribution of financial services products. They are assuming some of the basic roles historically performed by Wall Street. The current trend suggests that banks, not Wall Street firms as we know them today, will soon control the majority of retail securities sales, a tremendous portion of life insurance sales, and much of the financial planning that will establish the need for these products.

The reason for this shift can be summed up in a single word: Trust. Banks have historically controlled the savings dollars. Consumers perceive their bank as the place to save money, and for over 60 years no one has lost a dollar from an insured bank account. This sense of trust has transferred to bank investment products in the 1980s and 1990s.

The American baby boomer population is far more sophisticated about money than its parents. Today, nearly 80 percent of people in their thirties and forties say they need and want financial planning services; the vast majority of their parents never even considered using a professional planner to help chart their financial future. Leveraging their innate trust, banks which offer financial planning to customers have a nearly unassailable advantage over wire houses and other traditional investment product distribution channels. But it is up to the banks to deliver the goods to these avid customers; sophisticated financial services must become a core part of the bank for an increasingly sophisticated clientele.

Banks, which have already trained a generation of customers in the use of computer-assisted devices such as ATMs, also have a terrific advantage in the use of new technologies to serve a client base that feels perfectly comfortable using keyboards and video screens to conduct virtually every aspect of their lives.

And, just as banks demystified the complexities of interest yields on a vast array of depository products, they have an opportunity to simplify the pricing and marketing of mutual funds, annuities, unit investment trusts, and various types of life insurance.

The convenience that banks have offered customers—drive-through windows, branches in supermarkets, 24-hour ATMs at airports and malls—will increasingly be an important added value in providing financial services. One-stop financial shopping is upon us, and banks are leading the way. Technology will soon enable the next step—delivery of these services in the home through interactive television and computers.

As investment products become increasingly part of the core services of the bank, the cost to provide them will have to be more efficient to assure profitability. The question of disintermediation of funds has been largely resolved in the past few years. Most bankers realize it is better to keep a customer by making investment products available than to lose deposits altogether. Much more important is that disintermediation of customers slows dramatically when banks are able to meet virtually all of the financial needs of their clients.

Numerous surveys in recent years have demonstrated that customer retention is directly related to the number of products and services banks offer. *Bank*

Marketing Magazine reported that only 15 percent of customers using just one product at a bank were likely to stay with the bank for five years, but 80 percent of those using three products were likely to remain loyal. The Direct Marketing Association said the retention factor increased to 99 percent for customers using five services. These same studies indicate that customers who become and remain investment clients have better than an 80 percent chance of remaining with the bank for more than five years.

In this book, we devote a good deal of space to the need to go beyond merely offering a wide menu of financial products. Sound financial planning goes a long way toward creating needs-based services that are the key to truly enhanced relationships.

Another area of significant attention in this book is marketing. Selling alternative investment products has forced banks and their third-party marketing partners to adopt techniques and skills that previously were foreign to banks. Good marketing disciplines have enabled banks to understand and leverage a life-cycle approach to customers that takes into account purchasing behavior, savings habits, and other needs that have a direct bearing on the use of all other core products of the bank.

As we discuss each of these areas, we emphasize their impact on expense control, identifying specific customer needs, and providing superior customer service. We believe bankers will see how a strong investment program can help them address these concerns while reaping benefits of additional fee income and stronger relationships with retail and corporate customers.

Realizing that fee income is only a part of the banking picture, banks and investment firms which focus on this "back to basics" approach for their investment program are finding solutions which can be applied to traditional as well as nontraditional product programs.

CHAPTER 1

Bankers as Brokers: The Reality of the Business

The common wisdom for why banks got into the investment products business is that they wanted to earn the fee income. The reality is that most did so primarily for defensive reasons.

In the 1980s, record amounts of money were diverted from bank certificates of deposit and savings accounts to higher yielding mutual funds, annuities, unit investment trusts, stocks and bonds. Historically low interest rates on CDs and passbook accounts which couldn't even keep up with inflation were unacceptable to millions of bank customers.

Major financial institutions—primarily brokerage firms, insurance companies and mutual fund manufacturers which market their products directly to consumers—had launched an all-out attack on bank deposits. Bankers came to understand that deposit dollars, previously their domain, were leaking by the billions to other alternatives such as cash management accounts and money market accounts with checking.

Timing Is Everything

The arrival of third-party broker/dealers in the early 1980s, pushing many banks into the securities business, couldn't have been better timed. The economy was stagnant and interest rates were in freefall. If interest rates had gone up at the same time third-party brokers were getting established, they would not have been nearly as successful as they have been. For the previous 30 years, a safe bet would have been rising interest rates. But in the late 1980s and early 1990s, rates tumbled hard. There came a point when consumers had enough; they were looking for something else. Either a bank was ready with alternative investments or it wasn't; there were plenty of competitors out there willing to take the deposits off the bank's hands.

Bankers thus developed a defensive strategy that said, essentially, as long as brokerage firms and other competitors were trying to get into the banking business, their best response was to create a full range of financial services for themselves.

But, there was an unexpected consequence from this defense that is now revolutionizing the banking business. Bankers soon realized that in addition to helping stem the disintermediation of funds, the investment services they had reluctantly begun to offer were actually enhancing relationships with customers.

Bankers have always built their business through relationships with customers. As noted in the introduction to this book, the more relationships a bank has with a customer, the more valuable the customer is to the bank and the longer the bank is likely to keep the customer.

Bankers now realized that not only were their ties to customers improving when investment services were made available, but these alternative products increased customer retention. An investment product service provided another way for bankers to offer a one-stop financial service approach which enhanced the bank's value to existing customers and began to stem the leakage both of funds and the customers themselves.

A companion reason for banks to enter the investment products field is that it has allowed them to attract a different type of customer. By offering a value-added approach to meet the financial services needs of customers, they began to bring in customers who would both buy mutual funds and other investment products but also begin a more traditional depository relationship with the bank.

Fee income from investment products has become increasingly important as the programs become more mature. As profitable revenue generated by these programs increased, it earned more attention from senior management of the banks. And, as senior managers began to understand the unique sales and marketing aspects of investment products, they began to see the value of integrating these concepts throughout the bank. The result is an increasing number of banks which have developed an internal sales and marketing culture and mentality that is distinctly different from the "traditional" banking approach. For the first time, many banks began to establish sales goals and marketing-based incentive programs. Before investment products became commonplace in banks, most institutions had no need for sales motivation and sales goals. Because of the nature of the competition in the investment products business, banks were forced to adopt more of the cultural attributes of a sales-oriented business.

In the 1980s, most competition in banks was rate driven. As rates flattened out, banks have become more customer service driven. He who has the best customer service has the best customer retention and the best market share. If banks are not able to offer a quality investment products program, they stand to lose customers. The fear of disintermediation of funds has been replaced by a fear of customer disintermediation. Bank customers have plenty of other options to meet their financial needs so banks must use their strongest weapons—a full array of products and superior customer service.

The initial defensive posture has been replaced by a much more proactive embrace of the investment products business by banks of all sizes. The money center banks were the first to build this into their strategic plans. Such programs are ubiquitous in mid-sized and regional institutions and are extending into the smallest community banks.

Back to the Basics

As long as interest rates stay down, alternative investing in banks is going to continue to grow. When the trend reverses and rates go back up to the magic 10 percent or more, consumers will go back to buying CDs. But, because of customer service issues affecting customer relationships and retention, alternative products and brokerage operations in banks are likely to remain highly visible profit centers in institutions of all sizes.

One reason is that for a variety of structural reasons, the traditionally high margins banks have earned on deposits have been squeezed in recent years and may never rebound to the levels in the 1980s. As margins have become tighter, bank managements have focused attention on the most efficient ways to deploy their resources. The brokerage business, now established as a core profit center for many banks, is getting the same kind of management attention as checking, lending, credit cards, home equity lending and other contributors. As deposit/credit margins have shrunk, banks are relying more heavily on fee income than they ever have in the past. The trend is likely to continue.

A relative handful of major money center banks operate profitable broker/dealers *and* offer proprietary products. The majority of banks in this business rely on third-party marketers for these services and find they can leverage cultural and management resources gained in these partnerships throughout the bank.

In particular, banks that outsource these services to third parties will be able to drive fee income with very limited costs without incurring the expense of building and operating in-house infrastructure. Marketing skill is just one significant area of expertise the third-party firms have brought to banks which they would have found extremely expensive to acquire on their own.

Data used to implement target market approaches is more easily available today than ever before. We now live in a society that has the technology to compile electronic footprints about virtually every citizen. We know intimate details about the life cycles, lifestyles, habits of saving and spending and ways of living of virtually every individual. The third-party marketers have discovered ways of analyzing these footprints to determine with uncanny precision the names, addresses and telephone numbers of individuals who are most likely to buy an annuity or a mutual fund. This methodology is easily adapted to all bank products, including investments. As the retail bank learns more from the investment side of the bank about how to leverage these prime targets into all of its product sectors, the overall bottom line benefits enormously. More dollars are focused on a target market approach, and the result is a higher revenue yield per marketing dollar spent.

Among the first customers for bank brokerage and alternative investment products were the elderly. As their CDs came due and they realized they needed higher yields, they turned to annuities, mutual funds, and unit investment trusts to generate necessary income. Banks with well-run programs were able to meet the needs of these customers by leveraging the trust the customers had in an institution with which they had often done business for decades. While bank trust departments traditionally have handled the needs of elderly high net worth customers, the bulk of retired people need professional advice in managing lump sum distribution and setting up a lifelong revenue stream.

Today, every bank in America is working on a strategy to reach the baby boomer market, primarily because there are so many of them. Their income stream is becoming one of the highest for an age group in the history of the country. These consumers are dramatically aware of the effects of longevity; they see personal proof of it as their parents live productive lives well into their eighties and nineties. At the same time, health care costs and other expenses associated with longer lives continue to escalate. The baby boomers recognize the need for a much more focused approach to planning an economic future.

Investment products and financial planning services have value for many different customer niches, but for no segment are they more valuable than for baby boomers. A higher proportion of this demographic segment than any other group in history—79 percent—has indicated it wants and needs financial planning services. Some recent polls have indicated that the fear of dying is now exceeded by the fear of outliving one's income before death!

The media today has focused much more intently on financial planning and investing than ever before.

Years ago, newspaper columnists like Sam Shulsky or Sylvia Porter seemed to fulfill our need for "popular" financial advice. Today, sophisticated monthly magazines like *Money*, *Worth*, and *Smart Money* are found on the coffee tables of millions of baby boomers whose parents were happy to have read an occasional piece on retirement funding in *Reader's Digest*. Chapter 6 of this book provides more detail on financial planning services within banks and how they are the most valuable tool available for reaching the baby boomer marketplace.

Another major focus of the baby boom generation is estate planning. Older members of this group have accumulated some degree of wealth, but they are not trust customers of the bank. Their greatest need is preservation of their estate for their family in the event of an early death as well as making sure the estate will last as long as they do in the event they have a long life. Financial planning is a major need, particularly in finding ways of utilizing low cost dollars to finance high cost estate tax dollars.

Younger customers are also finding banks to be important providers of financial services. A 25-year-old college graduate just starting out on a career is not particularly concerned about retirement. But that person may need help in simply managing cash flow. We live in an era where people are much more comfortable going to consultants and counselors for virtually any kind of advice than previous generations. Banks need to be able to provide financial advisory services for these younger customers.

Increasing the Customer Service Focus

Financial services operations have had a significant impact on improving bank customer service overall, particularly if they include a strong financial planning component. Many banks have played with the idea of building a planning center internally. A number of serious questions must be answered, starting with the bank's willingness to deal with regulatory issues and liability questions raised by establishing such a proprietary center. In addition, financial planning requires a significant investment in highly skilled personnel with appropriate credentials, and spending for hardware, software and other fixed costs. Unless the bank has the opportunity to do a large number of plans—on the magnitude of thousands per year—outsourcing this function is the efficient route to follow.

Financial planning allows the planner and broker to look at the total asset base of a customer and to formulate a strategy to reach specific goals. The plan lays the foundation for the customer to build assets through cash flow or to reposition assets to meet specific goals. It also can provide a capital needs analysis approach which points to the benefits of life insurance. Customer service advantages are evident, and not incidentally so is fee income potential for the bank.

Utilizing the services of a third-party marketing firm that maintains relationships with a broad array of high quality insurance and mutual fund providers enables a bank to offer a strong lineup of household name packaged products. There are two benefits, not the least of which is the brand name value of strong mutual fund providers. By marketing well-managed mutual funds, the bank creates a vital layer of insulation from risk. Since many bank customers are first-time investors, the suitability of product is of primary importance. Over time, a professionally managed fund with a strong history of performance and clearly defined goals will almost always outperform any portfolio picked by an individual broker. Putting conservative bank customers in investment products subject to volatility would be very dangerous for the bank, exposing it to unnecessary risks and jeopardizing the assets of its customer. Professionally managed products recommended by a broker in a bank remove the bank itself from the line of fire in the event of poor performance.

Another subtle but valuable customer service benefit arising from a well-managed brokerage operation in a bank is the "rub off" effect for other bank personnel. A wise California banker once said: "Referrals are the internal combustion engine of a bank's success." A good third-party marketing firm will spend considerable time and effort educating bank employees on ways to improve customer awareness, not just of the investment products, but of all products in the bank. The average depositors will not utilize investment products services unless they are told about them. As platform personnel and tellers are educated on ways to identify potential investment products customers, they also learn techniques for cross-selling other retail banking products based on customer needs. Both the customer and the bank benefit.

A good third-party educational program will also educate bank employees on changes in the regulatory environment, new products and services and their suitability for specific kinds of customers, and marketing techniques that enhance the bank's overall approach to products and services.

Maintaining Control with a Third-Party Firm

One of the issues banks have cited most often for not wanting to be in the investment products business deals with a fear of losing control over an important aspect of their customer relationship. A bank not big enough to run its own broker/dealer is sometimes reluctant to turn over a customer to an investment representative working for a third party.

There should be little reason for anxiety if the bank maintains a strong degree of involvement in the selection of representatives who will work in its branches and if the bank's senior management takes an active role in the program. This role includes approving or improving marketing programs and materials, meeting regularly with the third-party marketer's representatives, attending CEO meetings put on by the marketer, and sending bank executives to the marketer for further education. If bank management is not comfortable with staffing or any aspect of its programs, the program will not be successful. If a high degree of comfort is achieved, the issue of control goes away.

The degree of control by the bank is also dependent on how much of the services of the third-party marketer it wants to utilize. The more services the bank utilizes, the greater the benefit it will realize through significant cost efficiency. Bank senior management involvement at every step is the best way for the bank to make sure it retains control over its own customers and the services being provided to them.

How does an institution decide whether to create its own broker/dealer or utilize the services of a third party? As will be discussed in more detail in Chapter 2, the questions banks need to answer deal with the cost of setting up appropriate financial planning, product selection, compliance, marketing, education and training, staffing, clearing, back-office functions, and the myriad of other tasks associated with the business. Perhaps more important is the question of risk to the bank. Appropriate reserves must be set aside for potential liability associated with recommendations, and a bank must be prepared to deal with an entirely new set of regulators, both state and federal.

Investment products—whether offered through an in-house broker/dealer or through a third-party marketer—have become core services for thousands of large- and mid-sized banks and a rapidly increasing number of smaller institutions. The term "alternative products" seems to be leaving the banking language, even for community banks. Today, about 8,000 banks are under $100 million in asset size and only 4,600 have more than $100 million in assets. The smallest community banks and thrifts have been prohibited from getting into this business until recently because they couldn't generate enough fee income to pay for the fixed costs of the business themselves.

No matter what the bank's size, to be cost-effective and profitable, these services should become a core product of the institution through a strategy that includes appropriate financial planning capabilities, the correct product mix and the ability to meet compliance needs. To skimp on any of these ingredients in bringing the services to market will stunt the success of the program.

While some banks will choose to have a direct relationship with a mutual fund manufacturer, there are three fundamental approaches which work best when banks deal with third-party firms:

1. **Traditional Relationship:** The bank and a third-party marketer agree on a pro forma that establishes realistic expectations for revenue, product mix, and fee income. Depending on the type of program, representatives may be employed by the marketer or the bank, and the level of other activities is fixed by contract.

2. **Community Bank Network:** A consortium is formed comprised of several community banks, usually under $150 million in assets, which operate within 100 or so miles of each other but are not directly competitive. Together they share the cost of a centralized operations center, a professional investment program manager, sales assistants and back-office activities, marketing, education, financial planning, customer data information, and all the benefits of a full-service brokerage.

3. **Correspondent Banking Program:** Very small banks, from $20 to $100 million in assets, can get in the financial products services by partnering with a larger bank, utilizing the tools of its program under a downstreaming concept that treats the smaller institution just like a branch of a bigger bank which is already a subscriber of a third-party marketing firm. The relationship is totally transparent to the customer, who receives customized statements from the third-party marketer. The smaller bank is indemnified through the larger bank.

New partnerships and strategic alliances are being developed. They will have an impact on both big institutions and community banks. More details on programs for smaller banks are provided in Chapter 8.

The Factors for Success

As the number of banks in the United States continues to decline through consolidation, and as the investment products business becomes more competitive, there will be fewer third-party marketers. Those that survive into the next century will be strong, well-capitalized and well-managed firms that offer banks everything they need to be successful in this business. The surviving firms will be the ones that offer exceptional value-added services to enable banks to meet their strategic needs for quality customer service, technology and expertise for exceptional marketing and administration functions, and cost efficiency through economy of scale.

Successful marketing of any product has always depended on identifying needs and solving problems. As the investment products business develops, bankers and their marketing partners need to be attuned to the changing needs of their customers.

Tomorrow's marketing basics may be totally unlike today's. Bankers cannot rely any longer on referrals alone to drive investment products. Great numbers of prospects who use banks today for traditional services are still unaware banks offer the investment products they want and need.

Investment products representatives in banks will increasingly seek out these customers through sophisticated target market prospecting that identifies potential investors with pinpoint accuracy. (Detailed descriptions of state-of-the-art marketing programs are in Chapter 4.) These same representatives will work closely with the corporate and mid- to small-sized business customers to establish pension, 401K plans and other investment programs for businesses with 10, 50, 100, or 200 employees. The cross-leverage of these kinds of relationships is remarkable.

The successful broker will be adept at using a laptop computer as a tool for presentations and financial planning sessions. Highly portable electronic communications capabilities will allow the representative to create comprehensive financial plans in the customer's home. A major focus for these value-added services will be computer literate customers who rarely enter a bank lobby today because they utilize

ATMs and other conveniences such as telephone banking.

The bank brokerage of tomorrow is already here. Those who recognize that fact and focus on a "back to the basics" approach will be the most successful in sustaining customer relationships, finding new customers with niche needs, and retaining market share in an increasingly fierce competitive environment.

CHAPTER 2

Building a Better Bank through Brokerage

What does a bank need to consider when deciding whether to build its own broker/dealer, selecting a third-party marketer, or forming some other kind of strategic alliance? Profitability and productivity are obviously major factors, but just as important are regulatory issues, liability and diversion of management effort, customer retention, and the selection process itself.

With sufficient revenue volume, it may make sense for a bank or bank holding company to create a broker/dealer. For the majority of banking institutions, however, renting brokerage from a third-party marketer makes more sense.

The main factors to be considered include the following:

1. The regulatory environment makes liability a major factor. A broker/dealer operation immediately opens up questions of liability for recommendations made to customers by its representatives. Due diligence and suitability are factors in every recommendation or transaction. A bank must have adequate reserves to address potential liability of judgments in favor of a customer who complains, either because of selective memory or actual misrepresentation or improper recommendation.

   The cost of protecting the bank's franchise from potential liability for compliance errors must be factored into any decision about whether to build a broker/dealer or "rent one" from an established third party. Risk to the bank's reputation must also be considered.

   An in-house broker/dealer opens the bank to multiple new sets of regulations administered by the Securities and Exchange Commission (SEC) and the National Association of Securities Dealers, Inc. (NASD) and, depending on the number of states in which the institution operates, the individual state securities authorities and insurance commissions. (Chapter 9 provides more specifics on compliance issues.)

2. Marketing expenses are high for investment products. To be successful you need to build a marketing department that is often substantially different from anything the bank has experience with. It requires staff familiar with investment

programs, developing motivational campaigns that have both creative flair and pass compliance hurdles, and use of technology to identify prospective customers.

This chapter will explain some of the advantages and pitfalls of both in-house broker/dealers and use of third parties. Our bias is generally in favor of the third-party route, for reasons of cost, insulation of the bank from risk, and superior customer service available through a top third party. If the institution has already decided to outsource the broker/dealer, selecting the right firm to provide those services can mean the difference between long-term success and mediocre productivity.

Setting the Standards

Before any effective due diligence can begin, the bank's chief executive, or an appointed task force, must conduct an introspective examination of the needs of the bank and its customers. The purpose is to reach a clear understanding of what the institution's goals and expectations are for the fee income program, how it is to be integrated into the general fabric of the bank, and how much time the senior staff can afford to give it.

When asked, most bankers say they entered the business for one of two reasons—either as a defensive strategy to retain market share against competitors or as an offensive strategy to build fee income for the bank. As outlined earlier, the reality is that most banks probably go into the investment products business for defensive reasons, in order to maintain strong customer relationships and retention rates. For this reason, the income generated from fees soon becomes a significant factor, and decisions made in the selection process can have a dramatic impact on how much money the bank will make over the long run.

By determining up front why they want to be in the investment products business, bankers eliminate the aggravation of evaluating a program later only to realize it doesn't serve the needs of the bank or its customers. Bankers must consider whether the short- and long-term needs of their customers will be met through an investment products program. As these programs have become more common in even the smallest community banks, disintermediation questions have fallen by the wayside and the banks have experienced stronger customer relationships.

Bankers must realistically evaluate the existing sales culture in their institutions, which may suggest a particular distribution strategy. Those institutions with a strong sales culture may find the best option is to license existing platform personnel to sell a limited portfolio of products distributed directly by fund manufacturers. Banks with a moderate sales culture may find it more appropriate to hire investment representatives who are licensed and registered through an outside provider. If the bank management has yet to embrace a sales culture, often the most effective approach is a fully managed turnkey approach provided by an outside firm.

Does the bank wish to have a full array of products and services available to its customers, or is it looking to add a particular type of product to meet a specific need? Just as no two banks are alike, no two third-party marketing firms are the same either. Some firms focus on annuities, some solely on mutual funds. Still others have a broad scope offering a wide variety of investment products and value-added services. Once the internal considerations have been evaluated, a checklist of the issues most important for bankers to consider will ensure they do not overlook any critical issues such as indemnification for the bank. In using the checklist, it's a good idea to set aside pricing considerations for the moment because far more important than the question of a few points of gross commission are issues that can have a dramatic impact on the bank, its customer relationships, and its regulatory posture. This checklist helps to assess all contenders equally when narrowing the field among multiple potential providers.

Some of the key areas to consider when developing this checklist include financial strength, experience, compliance, product depth and due diligence, implementation, pro forma analysis, incentive programs, corporate and field staffing and support, education, marketing support, financial planning, and information services and computerized order entry systems.

Financial Strength

When entering into any relationship with an outside firm to sell products to its clients, bankers must keep in mind they are putting the bank's reputation on the line. Before making what will amount to a long-term commitment to an outside provider, it is critical to know if that company has the staying power to serve the bank and its customer's needs for a long time to come.

Over the past few years, dozens of companies have entered this active arena, and inevitably there will be a shakeout as competition reaches its peak and as cyclical adverse market conditions take their toll. Since the investment products industry works within a cyclical environment with many peaks and valleys, the marketer must have the capital strength to survive in bad times as well as good. Further, it must have "deep pockets" and the ability to protect the bank from liability. It must have an established line of credit or a strong capital position. The vendor agreement should stipulate capital ratios which must be maintained. The time to consider these issues is not when a bank finds its partner has run into financial difficulties.

Experience

A bank will find the performance record of a partner under consideration of utmost importance with regard to operating in diverse market conditions and flexibility in meeting all of the bank's needs for today's market and beyond. While most firms do well in an up market, the question should be, has it competed successfully in an adverse market? Ask to see biographies of the key executives in areas such as product due diligence, compliance, education and training, marketing, account management, financial planning services, and execution and clearing. Ask for references from the firm's existing subscribers, and diligently check those references with probing questions.

Compliance

A firm with a strong compliance division can prevent many of the dangers banks face when making investment products available to their customers. To evaluate this, start with a review of the firm's standards. Ask for copies of the established compliance policies and make sure they stress the importance of following compliance rules and regulations in all aspects of the business—from suitability of recommendations through marketing materials—to prevent problems from occurring. Does the firm have the staff and other resources to provide compliance exams on all bank branches annually? Check the firm's track record. What is its history of winning or losing in arbitration? Call the National Association of Securities Dealers, Inc. (NASD) hotline (800/289-9999), and ask for a report on disciplinary actions. The North American Securities Administrators Association (202/737-0900) can provide access to appropriate authorities for similar checks at the state level.

Product Depth and Due Diligence

Does the third-party firm have a complete line of high quality products in its portfolio? Examine the list of preferred vendors carefully. If the firm focuses on a limited number of funds or annuities, it will not be able to offer the diversification necessary to assure customers have suitable investment portfolios. To learn whether there is a disciplined due diligence process, ask to see the review standards. Make sure the firm's staff includes qualified Chartered Financial Analysts. Chapter 3 has more details on due diligence standards.

Implementation

Having an established implementation team in place can eliminate many of the headaches associated with getting a program up and running. Ask to see a detailed list of tasks that need to be accomplished by specific people for a successful launch. To be truly successful, this task list should contain hundreds of items that take the bank from the signing process through start-up and beyond. It should also include the necessary systems and people for making everything happen. Bankers should learn who will be involved in the process and how many individuals will be committed to the bank through start-up of the program. The typical implementation process should take between 90 and 120 days.

Pro Forma Analysis

How realistic are the expectations for the new program? Many bankers have seen their programs fail due to unrealistic expectations about fee income potential or a projected product mix which is skewed to higher commission products not matching the needs of the surrounding community. A pro forma should be done based on objective goals established by micro studies of each branch. For banks evaluating a change from an existing program, the pro forma should be based upon an actual representative's production within their network versus a fictional example. The pro forma analysis should also include reasonable expense budgets. Beware of contenders who underestimate these costs in an effort to gain the bank's business.

Incentive Programs

Incentive programs should be available for both licensed and nonlicensed personnel and should be easily integrated into the bank's existing incentive program. Have the incentive programs proven successful in other institutions? There should be plans offering both monetary and nonmonetary incentives. Does the third-party marketing firm know the details of state regulation on compensation of licensed and nonlicensed personnel? Is there a recommended program for including investment products in the overall bank management incentive scheme?

Corporate and Field Staffing and Support

It is important for a bank to have easy access to the vendor's corporate officers and field support staff. How many individuals are dedicated to this support and how accessible is the corporate support staff? Banks on the West Coast may find it difficult to work with a firm whose support staff only keeps East Coast hours. To get a true picture of each firm, visits should be made not only to the home office of the partner under consideration but several clients should be contacted as well.

Education

Ongoing educational courses offered to both licensed and nonlicensed personnel are essential. Are these courses specifically designed to increase productivity in the bank environment? Is there a systematic approach to providing education—for the bank's platform and other personnel as well as registered representatives—to ensure consistency from one class to the next? Is there a means of tracking performance tied to the educational programs?

Marketing Support

There is a big difference between marketing with fancy point-of-sale brochures and marketing that offers comprehensive technology to define the market in precise terms and sales support to reach that market. With technology available today, banks should settle for nothing less than marketing support that gives representatives detailed profiles of prospective customers, even maps pinpointing the "hot pockets" where these customers are located. As the reservoir of customers from the existing client base of the bank dries up, there must be access to new prospects outside the bank. Ask for details on marketing support to help representatives reach their best prospects. Does the firm offer a variety of creative, motivational, compliance-approved materials appropriate to the bank environment on a regular basis? What type of customer seminar support is offered? Is there a program to integrate all employees of the bank into the marketing process?

Financial Planning

Banks offering financial planning services to its clients dramatically increase productivity and profitability with investment programs. Financial planning enhances a program by uncovering assets held outside the bank for investing and strengthening long-term client relationships. Make sure that the third-party firm has the ability to provide personal financial services, portfolio analysis, and retirement planning services for individuals and business customers. Are these plans prepared by professionals including Certified Financial Planners (CFP), Chartered Financial Consultants (ChFC) and Chartered Life Underwriters (CLU)? Does the firm provide these services free of charge to bank clients, or are they expensive options? One of the most valuable additional services a bank will offer its customers in the 1990s will be sound advice through a financial plan.

Information Services and Computerized Order Entry Systems

Strong programs require regular access to a range of product and sales performance information. Are sales presented by product in the bank as a whole, as well as by branch and by representative? Is there a source of funds report to tell the bank where investment money is coming from? Who does the third-party marketing firm provide this information to? Are there on-line information services for quick access? Does the computerized order entry system allow immediate access to customer accounts, or is it historical information? Can at least one year's history of client information be accessed through the system? Can the system be integrated with the bank's system? Data may be meaningless unless it is presented as useful, need-to-know information.

It should be noted that all of the above questions must be asked and answered for any bank considering setting up its own broker/dealer as well. They are the "bricks and mortar" for investment programs in banks, and without them, no program will achieve its potential.

After senior management has determined it will enter this business, the bank's commitment must be communicated clearly to other executives and staff, and the actual selection process begins. The most effective course is for the bank to appoint a three-person team to take responsibility for screening and selecting the marketing partner. But even after the actual selection process has been turned over to staff executives, the boss needs to stay abreast and show interest.

The task force begins by identifying priorities, objectives, and goals of the bank in establishing a preferred alternative investment program. They then establish a due diligence process, including a request for proposal (RFP) process for a short list of three outside vendors. Two of those firms should be invited to visit the bank. The selection team should also make on-site trips to the third-party firm's corporate offices as well as one or two current bank subscribers before a final selection is made. By visiting the third-party firm and meeting the professionals in charge of each area, the bank can be assured the necessary support services and infrastructure are in place.

A bank using a focused evaluation approach can complete the process from start to finish in approximately three months. With a clear understanding of the bank's goals and a focused checklist, selecting the right partner should be easy.

(For an in-depth checklist of third-party services, please turn to Appendix B, "A Third-Party Marketing Audit.")

Going It Alone

As noted earlier, if the bank wants to commit its own capital and pass the regulatory hurdles, it can build its own broker/dealer and have complete control over performance and profits. These banks must, however, consider several critical issues. The most important is that banks that construct broker/dealers assume all of the risk and will participate in an arbitration process if customers file complaints. The bank will be named in any consumer lawsuit and will have all of the financial risk of the litigation, including awards and legal costs. These "hidden" implications of operating an in-house broker/dealer unit should not be minimized, even if short-term economies may be neutral or even slightly positive.

As can be seen from the checklist above of essential functions, start-up costs for a broker/dealer are substantial. There is no standard time for how long it will take to get regulatory approval, and it is possible a bank might never be approved if it has capital problems or insufficient ratios. Months could pass waiting for regulatory approval to make the first trade, but the up-front expenses begin months before revenue starts to flow.

If a bank has a direct relationship with mutual fund manufacturers for packaged products which it then sells through an in-house broker/dealer, the revenue side of the equation is in pretty good shape, but the expense side remains high because of high fixed costs for back-office departments. For almost all banks, the most efficient combination to maximize profits is the sale of packaged products through a third party as broker/dealer. In the early 1980s, banks started out by renting brokerage. Some of the larger banks built their own brokerage and are happy with the results. But a number of fairly good sized banks have recognized the inherent problems and are coming back to third parties.

Expense and Efficiency

The costs to operate an internal broker/dealer can be staggeringly high. In fact, a recent study by Kenneth Kehrer Associates and DAK Associates shows there is a substantial difference in operating profits between bank broker/dealers and third-party marketing firms. The K² Study tracked the experience of representative banks in the $2.8 billion to $85 billion range and found, "Banks that use a third-party broker/dealer have investment programs that are twice as profitable as those that use their own broker/dealer. The difference in program profitability is largely due to the much higher operating costs of running one's own broker/dealer." One institution considering establishment of its own broker/dealer abandoned the project when its managers took a closer look at the cost to operate just one function, compliance. Each of its branches has to be annually examined by a compliance examiner who ensures that everything going on in the branch meets the standards of the National Association of Securities Dealers, Inc. (NASD) and the Securities and Exchange Commission (SEC). It would have cost the bank over $250,000 per year just to examine its branches. The allocated cost for a third-party firm to complete the same examinations was just $31,000, but in effect the bank paid nothing since the cost was built into the commission sharing arrangement.

Why such a dramatic difference? Both the third-party firm and the bank have to hire senior compliance staff, a fixed cost which one can spread over many institutions but the other must bear alone. Plus, the third-party marketer distributes the cost of its examiners over scores of banks and makes efficient use of their time and travel. An independent broker/dealer does not enjoy these economies of scale. Multiply this example by approximately 30 other functions or staffed departments to operate a broker/dealer, and the difficulties of achieving economies of scale in an independent broker/dealer are obvious.

Brokerage in a Box

On the other hand, a bank can rent brokerage, a service the third parties call "brokerage in a box." A third-party firm which already has regulatory approval can go into any bank today and put it in the brokerage business within a matter of 90 to 120 days, sometimes even sooner. The third party puts up the capital, takes the risk, and indemnifies the bank against loss.

Indemnification is the third-party broker/dealer's most valuable benefit. If an unhappy customer wants to sue somebody, he must sue the third-party broker/dealer. The broker/dealer pays the legal cost, not the bank. If a sales representative misbehaves and the representative's conduct causes the customer to lose money resulting in a lawsuit or arbitration, the broker/dealer is responsible. The third party loses money, not the bank, if a securities-related transaction finds its way to arbitration and there has been misbehavior. The insulation factor for the bank should not be underestimated; a bank doesn't want its good name tarnished.

Banks have a broad choice of relationships with third-party marketers. Every third-party company offers its programs in slightly different ways and with different names, but most firms offer four basic programs: managed, standard, platform, and hybrid. A brief discussion of each follows.

Managed Programs

A managed program, where the representatives and manager are on the third-party's payroll, is often used in states that restrict the sale of annuities and insurance products by bank personnel.

Third-party broker/dealers take all of the risks and do all of the work. They open the centers, hire and manage the representatives. Other than a commitment from senior management to make the program successful, the bank is required to do little except give the third party space in the lobby and access to its customers. The bank receives income off the top as a percentage of gross commissions.

From day one, the bank earns income without any expenses. If representatives work for the third party, they use its financial planning system, operate under a structured sales program, use marketing technology and materials provided by the home office, and report to professional managers. If the third party is first-rate, it is a successful process.

In a managed program, the third party commonly gives the institution 30 percent of gross revenues and keeps 70 percent. Series 7 representatives in managed programs get paid 30-35 percent of revenues. Managed programs have very high standards and representatives are expected to produce to specific levels.

Standard Programs

Some bankers prefer to take on more responsibility and earn more income with a "standard" program in which the sales representatives are "dual" employees. They are employed by the bank while their securities registration is carried by the third party. Although they are directed by the bank and supervised by the bank's registered manager, the third-party firm is held accountable for its conduct. Typically, in both standard and managed programs, the representative's full-time job is the sale of securities. It's all they do.

There are two major differences between a managed and standard program. First, whoever employs the representatives gets the biggest piece of the pie. Under a standard program where the representatives work for the bank, the bank gets the larger share of the revenue. From this revenue, the bank is responsible for compensating the representatives.

Second, in terms of supervision, important differences do exist. The standard program manager may be a banker, not an investment products executive, and the type of supervision may reflect cultural differences. In many cases bank managers don't require representatives to employ proven sales programs, hold public seminars, or utilize other tools provided by the third-party marketing firm.

In a standard program, the third-party marketing company keeps the small piece, 30 percent, and gives the bank the big piece, 70 percent. Theoretically, by the time the bank pays the representatives and fulfills other functions, it can bring more than 20-25 percent to the bottom line. Banks expect to make more money with a standard program, but it doesn't always work out that way. In reality, there is a differential of almost $90,000 in gross commissions per year, per representative between the managed programs and the standard programs. The bottom line is the third party knows what works and is more adamant about requiring that its sales program be followed to the letter. That's why productivity is higher.

Platform Programs

Managed and standard bank investment programs generate substantial revenue. Is there any way brokerage can be even more profitable? Some banks have opted for a "platform program" and it works, at least for a while.

Instead of hiring experienced representatives from Wall Street firms and paying them Wall Street prices, the banks take a new look at their existing bank employees—platform personnel already sitting in the lobby. Under these programs, in addition to opening checking accounts and handling other traditional products, they sell packaged investment products.

The platform personnel can be educated and licensed as Series 6 brokers and given a limited line of annuities and mutual funds to offer customers who come into the branch. Thus, they begin to capture the "walking-around money."

It is worth taking a closer look at platform programs. A dollar of fee income generated by the sale of investment product is divided three ways. About 35 cents goes to compensate the registered representative. Another 30 cents goes to pay for the "necessaries" which include legal, compliance, due diligence, and other fixed expenses. That leaves 35 cents as a contribution to the bank's overhead. For a bank to generate better margins, it needs to increase the 35 cents it retains, and the only way is to adjust compensation. Some banks do this by giving licensed platform people a "spiff" of 5-10 percent of the sales they generate. This can have a very dramatic effect on margins.

There is a downside. Platform employees sell investment products on a part-time basis. It's not their primary responsibility. They don't do comprehensive financial planning and they have a narrow knowledge of products. They also have a limited authorization to sell products with a Series 6 registration. More important, they are not natural sales people and don't know how to establish an ongoing relationship with customers. Their primary value is to handle the investable cash of customers who know what they want to buy. Banks can make a pretty good living on walking around money—for a while. Eventually, however, a more sophisticated marketing program is required with better trained and better motivated personnel to staff it.

Hybrid Programs

The industry is moving toward a more complex form of alliance between banks and third-party partners, a hybrid of platform and standard programs. It will be staffed by a combination of full-time Series 7 brokers who do financial planning and platform professionals who handle the walking around money. Platform programs are the industry's sales laboratory for these hybrids.

Under the hybrid system, brokers will supervise, motivate, and educate Series 6 platform people to be effective salespeople. Customers will go to the Series 7 broker for strategic advice and a detailed financial plan based on a comprehensive understanding of assets and their availability for repositioning. A platform employee is brought into the relationship and implements specific transactions based on the strategic plan. Financial planning by Series 7 registered representatives is the backbone of the whole process. The Series 7 broker will earn an override based on the success of the Series 6 people.

Hybrids are an excellent way to balance the scale because they offer the opportunity for a weighted average compensation system. Some sales will cost 35 cents on the dollar for broker compensation, but others will cost less than 10 cents on the dollar if platform professionals are involved. On a weighted average, representative compensation might be 20 cents without any sacrifice in service levels.

Some Other Considerations

Other important considerations include indemnification, arbitration, insulation from adversity, determining the source of funds, and compensation and performance expectations.

Indemnification

Of utmost importance, bankers must consider indemnification of the bank against any monetary or regulatory exposure with their investment program. An advantage of utilizing the services of a third-party provider is indemnification of the bank against any and all losses, claims, damages, liabilities, actions, costs or expenses which arise out of negligent, reckless or intentional acts or omissions of any third-party registered representative or manager.

Bankers considering any third-party marketing company must be absolutely convinced that the indemnification provision provided by the third party truly protects the bank and is written into its contract.

Arbitration

Whether the bank has its own broker/dealer or uses a third party, it is essential that the institution has confidence that its investment program is being run prudently. Consider the impact an arbitration case can have on a bottom line of a bank with its own broker/dealer. Suppose an organization does 300,000 customer transactions in a year. A fairly well-run program might generate 150 customer complaints. While this doesn't seem like a big deal—150 complaints out of 300,000 transactions is just .05 percent—it is only average performance in this business.

Nonetheless, suppose a third of those 150 complaints lead to arbitration, the investment industry's way of settling disputes short of a lawsuit. Assume that of the 50 arbitration cases, the bank loses 20 percent or 10 cases. When a broker loses an arbitration case, the customer is awarded the losses plus interest plus damages. Unfavorable decisions on just two or three cases could wipe out an entire year's profit for a good-sized bank program.

Because their profit margins are relatively slim, experienced third-party marketers conduct themselves in such a way that they avoid customer dissatisfaction. A substantial adverse judgment could wipe out profits and possibly sink a thinly capitalized marketer. At least the bank would not be obligated to pay for the legal defense or for any losses in this case. If a bank does business with an organization willing to take on such a considerable risk with narrow margins, it's a safe bet they are not operating in a careless fashion.

Insulation from Adversity

The bank that does not operate its own broker/dealer in effect transfers performance risk to a third party. Knowledgeable investors and brokers accept the prospect of adversity. When customers are unhappy with something going on with their account, who do they call? At the typical Wall Street wirehouse, unhappy customers call their broker. The investment world turns upside down in a bank. Who do bank customers call when they are unhappy with anything? Not infrequently, it is the chairman of the board or president of the bank! What happens to a broker by the fourth call the chairman gets concerning conduct in his lobby? Good third-party marketers will never allow the conduct of its representatives to jeopardize its relationship with the bank.

Successful representatives should not put themselves in a position of assuming performance risk. They should transfer it to somebody else. Bank management should discourage their standard program representatives from selling individual stocks and bonds. This helps to insulate the bank from adversity. The bank president or senior executive responsible for the investment program should receive a monthly scorecard of each representative's activity. If more than 20 percent of a broker's business is in stocks and bonds, someone should start asking some hard questions. The 20 percent level is arbitrary, because some unsolicited orders do come along and bank brokers do execute some of the bank trust department's trades. In general, if 80 percent or more of the business is in packaged products, management can relax.

Source of Funds

Bank managements should also be attentive to the source of funds being invested. Every transaction with a customer should include a report on whether the money came from a bank deposit or some other source. The source of funds report is a way of monitoring broker performance, showing whether investment money was cannibalized from the bank's own deposits. Nationally, 76 percent of all the monies *INVEST* handles come from outside the bank where the centers are located. For every dollar invested from a bank deposit account, an additional three dollars has been brought into the institution or under control from the outside. Bank managers should establish their own goals for this ratio.

Compensation and Performance Expectations

Bank executives have learned that if they want strong performance in their investment products programs, they must put compensation for those sales on par with other things done in the bank. Branch manager compensation packages should be based on deposits, loans and checking accounts, number of customers, etc., but also on the sale of packaged products and completion of financial plans. The integration of traditional and nontraditional program goals is a must for effective growth of the investment products business. One way to assure this is to make sure that job descriptions for platform personnel and tellers reflect the importance of leads and referrals.

In summary, bankers should understand all costs and implications involved in setting up a broker/dealer or renting this capacity from a good third-party provider. One such important consideration is indemnification to protect the bank. Whichever route they choose, they need to make a commitment to provide the proper support for all services necessary to make the programs work and to build the successful accomplishment of goals into job descriptions, performance reviews, and compensation packages.

CHAPTER 3

Due Diligence for Today and Tomorrow: Looking at the Products

In an extremely active regulatory climate the care with which banks select the products they sell assumes tremendous importance. But more important than the regulatory issues is the need for banks to assure that they present their customers with the best possible selection of products. The only way to meet both requirements is to institute a rigorous due diligence program that screens out unsuitable products and establishes a high level of comfort for the bank and its customers.

Product Selection Approaches

There are a number of methods that can be used in product selection including top-down, bottom-up, as well as quantitative and qualitative input. A multiple approach to specific recommendations is usually best by using a combination of filters to strengthen identification of sound investments with the goal of generating more achievable results.

Top-Down Approach

The top-down approach encompasses three distinct segments. The overall economic environment is the primary stepping stone to more specific analysis of both the fixed-income and equity markets. Interpretations involve, but are not limited to, a dissection of the elements composing gross national product, government spending, personal income and consumption, monetary policy, tax incentives, and the political and international environment and their relationship to current prices.

The second step is the analysis of long-term secular trends of both interest rates and the stock market. Interpretations can include such areas as the current position within historic norms for interest rates, earnings growth rates, price/earnings ratios, and dividend yields, as a whole, and by sector.

The third phase of the top-down approach involves identifying the shorter-term cyclical aspects of the securities markets. *INVEST* uses statistical, fundamental, and technical measures in the attempt to recognize changing trends in order to emphasize specific sectors or product types.

Bottom-Up Approach

After the overall investment environment has been assessed from a top-down framework, the bottom-up approach further segments the investment spectrum by relative sector attractiveness. On the fixed-income side, this encompasses taxable to tax-free relationships, the shape of the yield curve, and sector and quality spreads. On the equity side, this encompasses relative price/earnings multiples, growth, value, and earnings growth potential both domestically and abroad. Specific recommendations are representative of combined views of the best investments in the most attractive financial sectors within a forecast of the overall economic and market environments.

For specific recommendations, *INVEST* subscribes to traditional publications for both source and analytical material and has access to the views of its mutual fund and annuity vendors, their portfolio managers, and a vast variety of products they represent.

Quantitative and Qualitative Input

In addition to fundamental and economic developments, technical and quantitative factors should be used to both verify and complement findings. By adhering to those selections appearing favorable from all possible standpoints, the prospects for favorable results could be heightened.

Mutual Fund Product Selection

In the mutual fund sector, most banks rely on third-party marketers to conduct due diligence examinations of the products offered for sale. If a bank has a direct relationship with a mutual fund provider it must conduct due diligence of its own, and even if it offers only its own proprietary funds, someone within the bank must perform due diligence functions to assure that customer interests are being protected.

The process of selecting appropriate mutual funds begins with an inventory of the thousands of funds available to the third-party marketer or the bank. The challenge is to narrow the selection down to fund families that meet rigorous standards including the ability to meet the goals of the bank's client base.

The first step in the due diligence process is to contact the fund companies to be sure the fund is available for sale through the bank's distribution network. Generally, they will be glad to send a sales agreement and information about the fund. The sales agreement allows representatives to sell funds on a solicited or unsolicited basis, however, before the sales agreement is signed, numerous decisions must be made.

At this point, the due diligence focuses on the company itself, not the individual funds. How long has it been in business, what is the value of the assets under management, are there any unusual blips in their corporate history or any legal problems? Who runs the company and how long have they been in place?

In reviewing the history and current status of a mutual fund's distribution and management companies, assessing its ability to weather adverse market conditions to provide marketing support and to address compliance-related issues is important. Only mutual fund companies having the necessary capital to compete in the marketplace by adding new funds and maintaining others with limited expense to clients should be considered. Companies having subsidiaries or other businesses that could negatively impact the distribution or management companies financial capacity should be avoided. In addition, the firm and its key personnel must be free of regulatory or securities violations to meet compliance requirements. No third party or bank should sign a sales agreement with a company that has a history of poor performance, even if it intends simply to make its funds available rather than recommend them.

A marketer or bank should then select a short list of companies whose funds it generally feels comfortable recommending, what some call "preferred" vendors. Companies that make the list have a fairly broad base of funds that will qualify for active marketing, so that even within a single fund family customers can achieve a diversified portfolio of growth, international, government bonds, tax-free, or other equity and income offerings. This is called the "family" approach to mutual fund investing; the client should have a broad array of alternatives in the event either individual objectives or market conditions change. A variety of investments within a "mutual fund family" allows for diversification among product lines (fixed-income or equity), while providing the benefits of lower fees for combined purchases. To assure product differentiation, weight is also given to funds having a specialty market niche or superior expertise in a given sector.

The next level of scrutiny is the performance of the individual funds themselves. From the hundreds of products distributed by the vendors on the preferred list, it is best to pick the best five to eight funds in each major category. Selection is made by performance over five, ten, or more years. A younger fund can pass the tests if its manager has a proven track record and it meets all other criteria.

Within any category of funds, primary weighting should be given to above-average total return, generally within the top half of all funds with similar investment objectives as ranked by Lipper Analytical Services. Although emphasis should be placed on longer-term results when available, significant quarterly deviations from the norm should be carefully monitored. At *INVEST*, more than one quarter of unsatisfactory returns could result in lowering the rating from "recommended" to "approved." The difference lies in whether a particular fund may be actively solicited or one for which orders may be taken only on an unsolicited basis. Not every fund offered by a preferred vendor will automatically be recommended. If a fund greatly underperforms its stated objectives, or if conditions exist warranting consideration from a market timing point of view, *INVEST* may suggest a "sell or an exchange."

Bankers need to know in detail how their prospective third-party marketer performs its due diligence. Some companies simply say they will never offer a fund that doesn't rate at least four or five stars from Morningstar. The danger here is that relying on a single overriding criterion may cause excessive volatility in the list. Turnover is not good for bank customers, who get very uncomfortable if a representative recommends a fund one month and the next month sees that it has disappeared from the preferred list. Instead, companies should establish several important benchmarks which assure that the funds are good to begin with even though they may be subject to some cyclical changes.

It is important to know the education and experience level of product evaluators. Look for people who are knowledgeable about the brokerage and product distribution industries, with at least a bachelor's degree in business and finance and preferably an advanced degree in finance. A Chartered Financial Analyst has the right sort of credential, although you don't need a credential as much as a solid background in analysis of stocks or other securities, rather than in marketing or sales.

If the due diligence is done correctly, it should be just as hard for a fund to be removed from a preferred list as it was for the fund to make the list in the first place. A bank should ask how often the preferred lists change (more than a few new funds in a quarter should be looked at with some skepticism), and how the bank is informed of changes of all sorts, including dividends, management changes and other shifts. Is the bank informed on a timely basis and given a recommendation?

Bad things sometimes happen to good funds. In the event of adversity, what does the third party tell its representatives about how to reposition client's funds and other details?

Funds should be reviewed continuously, and updated information about recommended funds should be provided regularly to banks, including performance information on a latest-quarter, one-year, five-year and ten-year basis, turnover of portfolio, expenses, dividend changes and other information. Important information should be distributed to the field electronically on the day it is received, and extremely urgent information (such as removal of a fund from the recommended list) should be communicated both by telephone and written memo.

Evaluating Life Insurance Products

Banks will sell more insurance products in the years ahead, and for many of them selection of appropriate carriers is akin to stepping into alien territory. Skilled evaluators are perhaps even more essential in this area. Many bankers have a working knowledge of how mutual funds and securities are evaluated because their institutions have been in the trust business for years, but few have ever had to choose life, annuity, or other insurance products.

In the insurance business, the quality of the company is often a far more important consideration than the product itself. A bank or third party should decide on the specific insurance products it wants by determining particular features that have broad appeal to investors. These may focus on death benefits, stepped-up benefits, nursing home waiver and the like. Once the product has been identified, the evaluator can start looking at the firm itself.

Due diligence emphasis changes somewhat depending on the type of annuity products. A fixed annuity requires intense scrutiny of the issuing company. The evaluator examines documents such as 10Q and 10K reports of the company, as well as a Blue Book which lists all investments in the portfolio and includes a record of trades, maturity lengths, yields and other quality factors. A thorough due diligence effort will also include interviews with the issuing company actuarial staff to answer any question arising from the review of the paperwork. Special attention is paid to issues such as high-yield bonds, real estate holdings, mortgages, and futures and option related trades. A bank or third-party marketer should have established parameters of what it considers safe or unacceptable and all carriers must be in the upper 50 percent of the major ratings companies, consistently achieving scores of Aaa by Moody's, AAA by S & P or A++ by A.M. Best.

With variable annuities, the emphasis shifts more to the subaccounts than the carrier itself. In general, subaccounts that are not fixed accounts are totally segregated from the insurance company. Companies that offer fixed accounts within the variable product may have claims on the general portfolio. In this case, an evaluator must make sure the general portfolio meets the same established standards as the fixed annuity carrier.

The due diligence department of the bank or marketer monitors developments within all of the companies with which it does business as a matter or course. More detailed reviews depend to a large degree on how the major rating companies view firms at any given time. Insurance companies which have the equivalent of an A++ rating with little mortgage exposure and no junk bonds are reviewed once a year. Examination of quarterly 10Qs and other investigation of companies with lower ratings is required to make sure there has been no important deterioration that could impact customers.

In general, banks and marketers that have established stringent requirements for acceptability should see little need to remove insurance carriers for poor performance reasons. If standards are high to begin with, only the best companies will have made it on the preferred vendor list. This is important because customers may have to pay a surrender charge if the marketer or bank recommends they cash in a policy prematurely.

Doing It Alone . . . or Getting Help

Clearly, appropriate due diligence is a challenging and often expensive task, and only institutions with the infrastructure to support a staff of qualified examiners should attempt it on their own. Often in smaller or medium-sized banks, a bank executive is asked to perform due diligence along with his or her other tasks, and the result can be potentially damaging. Another solution is to hire an outside consultant to evaluate products and vendors. The consultant provides an independent voice which can protect the bank in the event of compliance questions, lawsuits, or arbitration.

Our bias, of course, is toward having due diligence done by a highly qualified third party which can provide additional insulation from adversity. If the bank is going to rely on an outside firm or consultant, it should make sure it chooses a resource with a clear record of objectivity, and that there are no actual or apparent conflicts of interest. The bank CEO or other senior manager should visit its third-party provider and check out the due diligence section, have an open discussion with the examiners, and see for themselves that the job is being done properly.

Going the Proprietary Fund Route

Among the growing investment product trends of the 1990s is the proliferation of new proprietary mutual funds brought to market by banks. By late 1993, some 107 banks had their own funds. The chief motivation was to be able to participate in management fees.

The biggest banks generate significant dollars in sales and can make a go of it. Their expense ratios are proportionate, and their funds will generate acceptable performance. But few banks of less than $1 billion in asset size can or should take the performance risk of bringing a proprietary family of funds to market.

There are four major issues a bank should consider before launching its own proprietary funds:

1. Will the fund be of sufficient size to permit competitive expense ratios? The performance rating of a fund is a derivative of the expense costs of operating the fund that are basically fixed. The larger the fund, the more expenses are covered. Often, there must be a considerable amount of seed money to bulk up the fund.

2. Banks will incur heavy marketing costs for the fund to generate sufficient assets for it to become competitive.

3. Can the bank afford to hire a top fund manager? The good ones require high salaries and benefits and competition is keen. The established funds have generally hired the best talent, paid them well, and given them exceptional opportunities for advancement as the number of funds from the name brand manufacturers continues to multiply.

4. Although many bank funds performed well in the low interest rate, bull market of the early 1990s, few proprietary funds have had to weather the storm of an adverse market. In a rising interest rate marketplace, asset values of bank funds will be affected, since about 85 percent of a bank fund assets is in income funds. As principal values diminish, banks are going to have some very unhappy customers on their hands. Since bank customers have never had to face diminished principal on funds they've in-

vested or deposited with their bank, the banks will be faced with defending a negative performance. Banks are looking at significant customer relationship risk.

Banks that operate proprietary funds are clearly taking on personal risk associated with their investment decisions and performance. They must be prepared to meet the challenge of potential customer defections that are directly related to the performance of the funds they manage.

A bank that is dissatisfied with the performance of a fund from a manufacturer can switch funds. A bank unhappy with the performance of its own funds does not have this option and must deal with a very upset customer. A bank with a proprietary fund may earn more in management fees, but does so at the risk of removing the shield that insulates it from blame in the event of adverse performance because it can't point to a third-party money manager outside the institution.

It is quite possible that somewhere down the line, a shakeout will occur if the proprietary fund expense ratios get way out of line or if results are not competitive with the established fund manufacturers and customer expectations. If this occurs, some will disappear and some may be taken over by traditional fund managers.

The surge in bank proprietary funds has invited scrutiny of the entire bank investment products industry by Congress, the OCC, OTS, and FDIC, all of which are proposing strong due diligence guidelines under which banks will have to operate, whether for their own proprietary funds or manufactured funds. The regulator's fear that the proprietary funds have created further confusion in the minds of consumers about what is or is not an insured bank product has added fuel to the debate over disclosure practices.

In general, only large money center banks with the ability to capitalize mutual funds of significant size should be in the proprietary fund business.

Considering the Private Label Option

An alternative, more cost-effective approach for banks to enter the mutual funds business is through a private label fund. In this case, a relationship is established with a professional money manager to provide the seed money to build mutual funds that are offered exclusively through the bank. In a private label mutual fund, the bank gets what it wants: participation in management fees. But a mutual fund company brings the fund to market, capitalizing and managing it with veteran portfolio managers who have track records. It is great for the bank, which benefits from someone else's capital. Banks don't get all the management fees on a private label fund, of course, but they do participate in those management fees with a lot less risk attached.

Products for Tomorrow

Over the past decade, bank investment products have been largely defensive in nature. They are designed to help banks maintain customer relationships and prevent customer defections. These products have offered asset growth and income potential to meet customer fears about the impact of retiring early and living longer. Insurance products have begun to include health protection riders and other benefits associated with longevity and an uncertain employment environment.

In the future, products will be designed to strengthen customer relationships with their banks. These products will most likely combine the best aspects of the current array of investment products in new versions which have more asset allocation attributes and which are designed to meet specific needs. There may be funds and investment products with actual dates on them—hypothetically, the "2030 Fund" could be designed for a person who will need to start taking out a specific amount of money in exactly that year.

There will be bond funds for emerging industries we have not yet heard of and new products, trusts, and annuity accounts in fields which did not even exist a decade ago. The need for strong due diligence to evaluate the worthiness of these new products will be greater than ever.

The investment product world is moving fast; customers are getting smarter and they learn about new products and strategies quicker. Banks and their third-party marketers must meet both of these challenges.

CHAPTER 4

The Marketing Secrets

Merely opening the bank's doors and putting up attractive signage will not make the institution's investment products business a success. The really profitable universe of customers may never have considered using their bank for investment products.

Bank marketing departments often devote significant time to research, usually focused on the Marketing Customer Information File (MCIF) or transaction history of existing customers. The number one question is generally: "What are our opportunities with existing customers?" The marketing department's information base is driven by the relationships they have with their own customers, and correctly so for the most part. This is important information but it does not describe what existing customers do outside the bank, what their total financial needs are, or where they are in their personal life cycle. This information is particularly important in the investment products area.

Bankers have historically focused on the credit side of the business to generate income. There has been relatively little need until recently to learn where a customer's major assets lie. Many bankers would be surprised at the findings of recent studies which show 80 to 90 percent of a customer's assets are held outside their primary bank. If a bank only handles the customer's checking account, loans, and credit cards, it often won't know about these other assets.

Banks, like other businesses, often do not take care of their best customers or seek out people who could become good customers. Many bank customers and prospects are undersold and undercontacted. Bankers often do not have a clear picture of the amount of financial services business these people are doing elsewhere. Lew Young, former editor-in-chief with *Business Week* was quoted by Tom Peters in *In Search of Excellence* as saying, "Probably the most important management fundamental that is being ignored today is staying close to the customer to satisfy his needs and anticipate his wants. In too many companies, the customer has become a bloody nuisance whose unpredictable behavior damages carefully made strategic plans, whose activities mess up computer operations, and who stubbornly insists that purchased products should work."

The successful bank brokerage operations have borrowed heavily from the marketing disciplines of the consumer products sector. Their success demonstrates that the biggest responsibility of bank marketing is to define targets in precise terms both inside and outside the institution, devise a strategy for understanding what these people need, and then reach them with sales messages for products which satisfy those needs.

A good place to start is for bankers to begin viewing their bank branches as retail stores with fixed employee and operational costs. Every square foot ought to be actively used to sell something to customers who come in every day, or to reach out to those customers who do not regularly visit the "store." Seen this way, a bank becomes an outlet and a distribution center for financial products and services that meet customer needs. But, if we don't understand who the customer is, our retail store may stock the wrong products. For example, a bank might offer only products which complement its operational systems—a certain type of checking account or home equity loans structured in just one way—and the customers must take it or leave it. More often today they'll leave it.

One of the findings of a recent Investment Company Institute survey illustrates a new trend moving to the forefront of consumer needs: 79 percent of baby boomers acknowledge they *want financial planning*. Bank marketers may find that addressing this and related needs of the baby boomers may be the most significant marketing opportunity of the 1990s.

We live in an age driven by technology, so it is not surprising that the most effective bank marketing initiatives use powerful technology to maximize fee income. The steps begin with a definition of the bank's market in precise terms. Next, it must convert the information about its market into applications to be used at the representative level. Finally, technology can be used to deliver remarkably effective needs-based information and point-of-sale materials.

The essence of the first step is to be able to identify actual customers and prospects within a specific branch trading area. A bank can utilize existing technology to precisely identify who lives in its primary market and what their propensity to buy specific products will be. Such branch trade area studies generally focus on the 1.5-mile radius most banks claim as their primary market. But the studies are flexible as to actual geography covered, because in reality, many of a bank's customers live beyond this commonly used distance. The goal should be the ability to isolate and analyze specific areas down to sectors with as few as 10 to 15 households. The more narrowly defined the trade area, the closer banks and brokerage representatives can get to precisely defining the customer.

Who Are the Customers and What Do They Buy?

Everything a banker needs to know about the customers in the primary trading area should be condensed into a single branch marketing strategy report which gives a profile of who lives in the area, how much they have to spend, where they are in their life cycles, and whether they are likely to buy mutual funds or annuities. The elements include profit potential, additional marketing details, and identifying customer needs.

Profit Potential

Any bank that wants to be successful with investment products sales should develop branch profit potential reports. Marketing technology available from *INVEST*, for example, includes a proprietary revenue forecasting formula that combines demographic information with specific deposit balances and the number of accounts within each deposit type. This forecasting method predicts how much fee income a branch will produce in a 12-month period with an 85 percent accuracy rate.

What is the value of knowing how much fee income a branch can do? The bank then knows which branches to focus on, the number and type of representatives a branch can support and, objectively, how to set realistic sales goals.

Let's say a bank has three branches in one area. The forecasting model indicates that none of the branches could support a full-time representative, but one branch has a larger fee income potential than the others. This site then becomes the home base where the bank actually houses a representative, and the representative drives to the other branches one day each week to cover its needs.

Not too many businesses in America can know the profits they will produce before the front doors open. Existing marketing technology allows banks to do this with every branch with estimated revenue forecasts based on a proven algorithm, not by the seat of the pants.

In fact what such studies will show is that not every bank in America should be in the investment products business for the profits alone. Some regions don't have the proper demographics and deposit mix to produce meaningful revenue. There may be other reasons to go forward with a program—providing a service that is vital for customer retention, for instance—but the technology will tell the banker in advance whether investment products themselves will generate a profit.

For most banks, revenue forecasting provides an objective foundation for goal setting, planning, site selection, and staffing. If these are overstated or underestimated the credibility of the program can dramatically diminish with senior management as well as the sales force.

Additional Marketing Details

By analyzing the demographics of the branch trade area, banks can learn where potential investment customers are in their life cycles, which helps indicate purchasing propensity. As indicated in Exhibit 4-1, meaningful information can be extracted to break down the trade area according to age and median household income. Area growth projections will show whether there are likely to be more or fewer customers in years ahead, which is important for a bank to know as it locates its investment centers. Another key indicator is the ethnic mix breakdown, which is important in analyzing the different needs of existing and potential new customers, with regard to staffing on specific holidays, scheduling seminars, determining product needs and point-of-sale set up at the

**Exhibit 4-1 Branch Marketing Strategy Report
Age and Income Information**

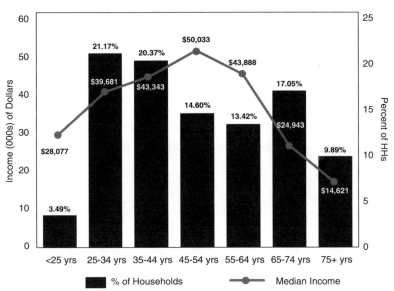

branch. Recognition of the specific needs of ethnic groups is imperative in today's marketplace.

Identifying Customer Needs

A good market profile will precisely define existing and potential customers from a marketing point of view and what their specific needs are. Banks cannot learn this if they study only the MCIF, which is transaction-driven, not needs-based. The MCIF is, however, an extremely important tool in understanding the full relationship banks have with their customers.

Investment behavior is primarily determined by position in the life cycle. Exhibit 4-2 lists three separate client categories, made up of "Achievers," "Prime Earners," and "Retired." The exhibit clearly identifies their likely portfolio goals and concerns as well as products and services to offer people at different stages of the life cycle. Achievers, the younger group, are credit-driven and have goals of accumulation. Prime Earners are maxing out their income levels and have portfolio goals of enhancement. And the Retirement group wants to enjoy life and has portfolio goals of preservation. Investments are driven by these three life cycles.

Few banks under $1 billion in assets have this information at their fingertips or the resources and marketing staff to produce it. Since it is valuable and necessary information, they sometimes buy it but often do not have the experience to work effectively with it. The best third-party marketers will not enter into any arrangement with a bank which does not allow a study of its branches, branch by branch, on a micro basis. How can the marketer recommend what type of program to run without understanding the profit potential or the customer's needs? Profiling bank markets in precise terms makes the third party a more effective marketing colleague.

Tapping into a Wealth of Quality Information

There are many sources of basic demographic information—census data, ZIP+4 household data, numerous market segmentation systems like MicroVision-50 from National Design Systems, and of course the

Exhibit 4-2 Life Cycle Needs

Segments	Age Range	Portfolio Goals	Concerns	Products	Services to Offer
Achievers	25-44	Accumulation	Income Tax Reduction College Funding Building a Career Buying a Home	Variable Annuities Growth Mutual Fund Auto Loans Mortgages CDs	College Planning Systematic Investments Financial Planning
Prime Earners	45-64	Enhancement	Income Tax Reduction Retirement Planning Convenience/Time College Expenses	Tax-Free Funds Growth Mutual Funds Income Mutual Funds Annuities (Fixed/Variable) Home Equity Line of Credit Mortgages CDs	Retirement Planning Portfolio Review Lump Sum Distribution
Retired	65+	Preservation	Income Taxes Preserving Lifestyle Interest Rates/Income Estate Taxes	Fixed Annuities Tax-Free Funds Income Mutual funds CDs	Estate Planning Portfolio Review Comprehensive Plans Lump Sum Distribution

bank's own MCIF. Usually a combination of these information resources works best. The challenge is setting up an effective matrix to analyze and manage the huge amounts of data generated so it becomes useful information generating action. New technology is applied to sort the information and paint a clear picture of branch profit potentials, site selection, general customer profiling, and what products complement the customer's needs.

There is a danger if demographic data is viewed just from a bankwide (macro) perspective. When the institution has many locations spread throughout different neighborhoods and demographic areas, this perspective can provide a misleading profile of the best areas for new customer prospects. Each individual branch location should be profiled with its own microstudy. Only then can bankers clearly see the profit potential for nontraditional as well as traditional products at each branch and predict the commissions as well as cross-selling opportunities likely to be generated at a specific branch.

Through use of a microstudy followed by a macrostudy, bankers will be able to identify and target prospects in their branch trade areas who have a high propensity to invest. This information forms the basis for a comprehensive integrated bank marketing plan which emphasizes drawing power, selling power, and the motivation of both customers and employees.

Banks habitually mass-mail information they want the public to know about. A 10,000-piece or 50,000-piece mass-mailing is not uncommon. But how can banks know which potential clients in a marketplace have the highest propensity to make two or more transactions on the investment side in a year?

A wealth of relevant customer information exists today and is available to banks from data companies. These firms access information from a myriad of sources. For example, some supermarkets give check-writing customers an encoded identification card. After all their groceries are electronically scanned, priced and recorded, the last thing the check-out clerk does is swipe customers' ID cards across the scanner. With this simple step, the supermarket is profiling everything. When the supermarket gave out those cards they captured the customer's name, address, age, Social Security and driver's license numbers and everything demographically significant about the person. This data, for example, can tell the marketers that a married male, age 33, shops on Tuesdays and Fridays because the supermarket records the dates he comes in. They know everything he buys and can accumulate, massage, and evaluate the data until they know exactly what he did in the store today and will most likely do tomorrow.

The big video chain stores collect similar information every time a customer hands his video rental card to the clerk, and so do oil companies and department stores. A bank or its third-party marketer can license this information from the data companies, cross-referencing and correlating it to determine purchasing habits that indicate what members of a specific market group looks like from an income standpoint, what they buy, what magazines they read, what videos they rent. The challenge is to renew, analyze, and update the information available continuously to assure quality, "need-to-know" information, and then to apply it to learning which prospects are likely customers for mutual funds, annuities, or other financial products.

Converting Information to Action

In the 1980s, increased bank lobby traffic was straining people and resources. To reduce operating costs, banks started an all-out initiative to move their customers out of the branch lobbies, using tools such as ATMs, drive-through windows, direct payroll deposits, and electronic banking. Machines, able to do most transactions at a fixed cost without health or other benefit expense, were cheaper and more efficient than people. Additionally, the busy lifestyles of the baby boomers invited time-saving devices. Traffic in the lobbies, however, has been reduced to the point banks in the 1990s began using innovative marketing techniques to entice customers and prospects back into the lobbies.

With escalating marketing costs and an ever increasing number of niche groups with diversified needs, it is obvious the conventional methods of mass advertising for most banks would not be efficient. The better third-party marketing firms have worked with banks to develop targeted, cost-efficient methods of rebuilding traffic in the branches and attracting new banking prospects. A principal weapon has been resourceful and cost-efficient use of direct mail and seminars to reach targeted niche groups.

Over the years, the poor performance of direct mail programs in the industry had created strong negative biases about them. These prejudices were driven by three main concerns:

1. The direct mail lists were often outdated and improperly maintained, and banks were receiving up to 25 percent of their mailing pieces back due to change of address, death of the prospect, etc.

2. The lists were not profiled to meet the niche group the marketing was targeted to. For example, a retired couple might receive a college funding package, resulting in a wasted mailing contact.

3. Banks and their representatives received the same list as everyone else, so prospects were bombarded with similar offers.

To resolve these issues, *INVEST* developed a proprietary direct mail prospecting program for client banks called INVESTLINK℠ which differed from previous prospecting systems because of several unique features.

Profiled lists. All names on the lists received through the program are of people who have been profiled on their propensity to buy mutual funds and annuities. The system gives priority to high-demand ZIP codes.

Private lists. The prospecting list the representative receives is exclusive to a single representative—no other subscriber bank in the area or its brokers will receive these names for at least 12 months.

Clean lists. To assure they are clean and solid, the files are scrubbed and updated 65 times per year with a 95 percent successful delivery to the intended prospect.

Prospecting Programs

A good prospecting program should target large or small groups of prospects and be easy to use. The program should include a number of critical components, beginning with a prospecting tool for *attracting new customers* to the bank by generating names of people fitting the profile of an annuity or mutual fund customer with a high propensity to buy. Such lists can also be used to build awareness of a bank's name (especially helpful after a merger or acquisition), a branch opening, or to introduce a new investment center or other new products or services.

One element missing from most bank prospecting programs is how to insure representatives know which list of names to order. *INVEST* has solved this dilemma by providing a market index pinpointing high demand areas within each marketing area. The representative receives a complete analysis of the bank branch's county broken down by ZIP code and displayed on a color-coded map. This is an easy way to chart an effective strategy for using the system and it tells the representative exactly where to invest his time and money.

The second element of a good prospecting program is a system that allows the bank or representative to *leverage existing customer relationships.* The system used by *INVEST* enables a bank or representative to submit an investment client's name and address and get back a list of the customer's 30 closest neighbors who are likely to have similar income levels and lifestyles. It works on the principal of "birds of a feather flock together." The key benefit is the representative has a manageable list and has already been successful selling in the neighborhood.

Banks can also profile their existing customers and isolate those who have a propensity to buy annuities or mutual funds by using a unique proprietary program for this purpose. This same lead generation program can also be used to produce profiled lists of the most desirable nonbank prospects in the bank's service area. A unique feature of the program is that it allows the bank to personalize its approach to its existing customers and to potential prospects and can reduce direct mail costs by over 60 percent.

Beyond individual customers, marketing technology is now also used to provide banks with lists of small- to medium-sized businesses that fit specific profiles and are candidates for pension services. *INVEST* has developed a comprehensive sales program which, in addition to supplying the names and addresses of the companies, provides a "how-to-get-started" approach for the bank. It includes all the sales materials a representative will need including compliance-approved letters to send to executives of the target businesses and an information gathering process for the sales presentations.

A good prospecting program should also include all of the direct mail fulfillment materials and recommendations on how best to utilize it. These materials include:

- Prospecting letters
- Brochures
- Order forms
- Direct mail timetables
- Awareness building ideas
- Prospecting tips
- Free financial planning certificates
- Toll-free customer service number
- Seminar recommendations
- Prospect mailing list and pricing
- Direct mail follow-up program

It is still rare to find a fully integrated direct mail prospecting program offering research, a selection of programs, "hot spot" identification of prospects, profiled mailing lists, and a comprehensive fulfillment package. But they are fast becoming an essential component of achieving the key priority of generating new footsteps in bank lobbies.

Once a bank secures a powerful lead generation program, it needs to provide its sales representatives with methods to assure success. The two go in tandem. Representatives who follow clearly defined steps for reaching and maintaining contact with prospects have higher response rates because they are carried from the introduction through to closing the sale in a face-to-face appointment in the customer's home or in the bank lobby. A number of such programs exist. The only secret is to make them a way of life for all bank representatives to follow.

Some Proven Techniques

Marketing support shouldn't end with direct marketing. The plan must include a full range of motivational materials including point-of-sale pieces, seminars, ads, statement stuffers, prospecting letters, scripts, and public relations activities to motivate prospects to invest. The word advertising itself comes from the Latin *ad vertere*, meaning "to turn the mind toward." Therefore, any campaign should motivate the customer to buy. Many campaigns are quickly forgotten because employees throughout the bank were not also motivated to sell.

The style of the campaign must capture attention and its theme must be based upon addressing the needs customers currently have that the bank can serve, rather than selling particular products. Bank marketing campaigns should include tools in three areas: 1) to increase their sales and productivity; 2) to help promote branch involvement; and 3) to focus representatives on a specific marketing campaign for a set period of time.

Representatives should have a four-month calendar suggesting what to do each month. Their job is to implement campaigns and strategies, not think them up.

The same campaign should go to all representatives and bank marketing departments so they are all on the same page at the same time, telling the same story, and using the same sales materials. Try to give everyone everything he or she needs and provide as much written communication as possible to help in implementation. New marketing campaigns should go out every four months, always promoting a new theme, with marketing kits designed to motivate and integrate within the entire bank.

Integration is very important. Search for a vehicle to get the bank's nontraditional elements aligned with its traditional side. If the bank's culture is just starting to pick up on a new sales orientation but it still takes orders in a passive manner, theme campaigns help them become proactive and to integrate alternative investment products into the banking environment bringing everyone together.

Statement stuffers, product information, profiling information, seminar scripts, balloons, tent cards for desks, direct mail pieces, reply cards, point-of-sale materials, should be provided. Advertising should address free financial planning. One firm includes a letter from an economist talking about issues of concern in a given quarter, such as taxes or college tuition.

Advanced education and recognition of each employee as an individual is a powerful motivating force and is vital if a bank wants everyone to maximize referral potential for annuities and mutual funds. Where strong referral programs are in place, the bank's cross-selling ratios of traditional products have increased.

Campaigns are designed, in subtle ways, to disturb the client. Any marketing campaign worth implementing will discomfort, disturb or create a question with the client in a nice way. If it doesn't, if there is no call to action, everyone is wasting time and money. Here are a few examples of successful campaigns:

"Just Ask"

If tellers wear "Just Ask" stick-ons, customers have to inquire: "Just ask what?" That's a call to action. Banks can promote checking or loans and investments. When this program was introduced recently, banks were told they could use everything provided in any manner they choose, in the lobby, in seminars or in bankwide meetings. It became a huge success and is now part of the implementation process for new client banks.

"Take a Tax Detour"

"Take a Tax Detour" was designed as a way to provide banks with promotional ideas to use in the entire branch system encouraging customers to reposition assets to minimize tax consequences. It provided posters, collateral materials, stickers, advertising, and most important, a bank could use it for traditional products as well. Tax seminars promoted through the "Tax Detour" campaign are one of the hottest investment sales tools. All seminars should be educational and should not promote the bank or a specific product. Twenty-five percent of those in attendance request follow-up appointments, a very strong statistic for any marketing program. Baby boomers, especially, want more information.

"Nobody Plans to Fail, People Fail to Plan"

Working off the old adage that if someone doesn't care where they're going, they can take any route to get there, seminars on financial planning can be very successful. The seminars help people understand how to reach a particular goal through planning. Customers are encouraged to sit down with representatives and discuss their goals. Representatives hand out financial planning samples and point-of-sale materials to get people interested and excited about financial planning. The response rate is generally excellent.

"The American Dream"

American Dream seminars show people how they can still attain the American Dream. Banks begin with a lobby campaign in which customers can win a savings bond by answering two simple questions focused on savings and investments as an excellent lead generator. The next step is an invitation to a seminar or to meet with a broker. The American Dream concept reaches the deep inner feelings we all aspire to and raises the awareness level for financial planning.

These campaigns have similar elements—they focus on needs and they are constantly changing. Marketing staffs must always be aware of the changing needs of the consumer.

Achieving Management Buy-In and Educating the Team

A complex puzzle facing bank marketers is how to sell in an environment that historically has not put sales in the lobby as a priority. The question most often asked is, how do you bring it all together and make it work?

To be successful, the marketing team must get senior management's "buy-in" for a program which includes recruiting virtually all employees of the bank to become part of the retail selling effort. If the marketing plan does not have senior management's full support, it should not go forward because it is likely to fail. Once management gets behind a well thought-out campaign, it can be implemented through motivation and building excitement. Top management must be a part of kick-off promotions and incentive events. They must reinforce the value of the program through memos and correspondence with employees and visibly express its support for the programs as ways to motivate employees. Management must be unified in its commitment to insure success of any program. One negative reaction by a member of the management team can kill a program.

One of the best motivators is education. One reason so many platform employees are reluctant to support the program is usually a fear of something they don't understand. Bank employees from senior management through all levels need to be educated about a marketing campaign before it is launched. By understanding the corporate goals of the campaign and the value to the bank and its customers, employees can be the program's biggest promoters.

A good benchmark would be to allocate 30 percent of a campaign budget to educating employees and providing incentives. Without this level of support programs often fall short of great expectations.

Successful programs often benefit from including the customers themselves in the marketing effort. To get customers enthusiastic is the ultimate selling tool because there is nothing like a genuine testimonial from a neighbor or friend to convince a prospect a bank has good products or services available. By including some element of "pride of ownership," the customer gains bragging rights and the bank now has a built-in referral network.

To sum up, various state-of-the-art programs and technology are available to help banks position investment programs, to show representatives how to identify their prospects and the newest ways to reach them. But more important than leaping into these technologies is understanding how to make them part of a total marketing solution. The hub in the wheel of marketing technology is quality information and knowing how to use it. To reach its maximum potential, a sound investment program must be based on current, accurate and easy-to-use data drawn from reliable sources and assembled in a user-friendly form.

A strong program must generate an action plan. The basic information has been analyzed, the branch locations selected and representatives installed. The challenge of finding a customer and presenting an appealing message based on need has also been positioned by technology. This is all leveraged by a variety of selling techniques, such as seminars, incentive programs, and other elements in the total marketing solution.

Finally, when management buys into the marketing program, and all employees and even customers are made to be a part of its success, the bank investment program will reach its full potential.

CHAPTER 5

Everyone Back to School

Absolutely essential to a successful investment products business is the trust customers have in their bank. By definition and strategy, bank investment programs should not offer high-risk investments or securities that do not match bank customer's conservative investing philosophy.

The sale of annuities, mutual funds, unit investment trusts, and life insurance is becoming commonplace in banks, complementing traditional product lines. But even the most conservative of these products are not insured deposits. As banks offer these products to customers, bankers and selling representatives must be taught to protect the trust inherent in the bank. It is primarily up to the investment representatives to learn how to work within a bank culture which has a traditional and well-defined way of doing business. It is up to the representative and bank managers to learn how both "cultures" can benefit from their mutual strengths while integrating their efforts. Accomplishing these goals requires:

- Educating investment representatives to "manage their method";
- Educating bankers to understand the investment products business;
- Constructing a "referral machine" within the bank to send business both ways—to the investment side and the traditional products; and
- Maximizing customer service through financial planning.

This chapter focuses on educating representatives and bankers. Most of the examples are drawn from our experience. Although similar programs exist in one way or another at other quality third-party firms and banks.

Education, Not Training

A few years back, our firm stopped the practice of "training" representatives and bank employees and focused on education. The subtle language difference is a clear statement of our goals. We changed our representative courses. We added platform representative instruction and education for sales assistants. People who were not even considered part of the process in the past are now empowered by education.

The culmination of this philosophy is the founding of *INVEST* University, a state-of-the-art program that will surpass all other methods in efficiency and thoroughness.

The goal of any bank investment products educational process should be to take raw potential and produce productive skills. Not everyone is well-suited to the job of selling investment products in banks, and those who are not will inevitably cause problems for the bank. A good education process acts as a filter.

Education is an essential value-added service of a third-party marketer, and banks should learn everything possible about their potential partner's program before signing on. Education keeps representatives as well as senior bank management current on the various aspects of the investment products delivery system, how to achieve success, and how to integrate brokerage with the retail banking delivery system.

There should be six major initiatives in a successful education program. These include classes for representatives, platform representatives, advanced sales, managers, sales support productivity, and bank associates.

Representative Class

Although investment representatives and managers obviously get instruction on products and services to obtain the appropriate license, their education must be expanded to address the unique challenges of investment services within a bank. The foundation for all investment representative educational programs must be long-term, needs-based relationships with customers. Programs should emphasize techniques of working within the bank environment and understanding the importance of the high level of trust people have in banks.

Successful investment representatives learn to "manage their method"—understand the dynamics of the bank environment and take planned steps to conduct business in response to these dynamics. Many representatives have done investment sales in the past. They come from traditional brokerages, insurance, or financial planning organizations. It's critically important to modify their behavior, expectations and philosophy to learn behavior appropriate for a branch lobby and how to open and maintain a dialogue with bank and branch personnel. At *INVEST,* these representative classes are conducted in our headquarters in Tampa. Although banks assume some of the travel expenses, there is no charge for the education itself.

Platform Representative Class

Special classes are held for bank platform personnel who work in programs where bank employees combine the responsibilities for traditional banking services and brokerage into one job. The platform representative class is for Series 6 representatives and it is conducted on-site wherever the institution is based. These sessions last three or more days and reflect the individual bank's culture. Follow-up sessions are held a month after the classes and reinforce what was learned.

Advanced Sales Class

Courses are designed to increase the productivity of experienced Series 7 or Series 6 representatives. Potential topics include all aspects of being a representative, such as goal setting and advanced presentation skills. These classes are scheduled on a periodic basis depending on the specific needs of the representatives and are held on-site at the bank's offices.

Manager Class

Designed just for investment program managers, this three-day class is conducted in Tampa once a quarter and is a requirement every program manager must fulfill. The major objectives are to deliver the most up-to-date information on investments, compliance, operational, and administrative procedures as well as to work with them on management skills. Techniques are taught on running sales meetings, motivating employees, handling performance reviews, hiring and firing, and creating an ethical environment.

Sales Support Productivity Class

Sales assistants supporting the representatives in the field are taught time management, administrative skills, compliance, and operational requirements. Sales assistants should be included if a representative or a group of representatives does more than a minimal level of business because having an effective sales assistant leverages their time and increases productivity.

Bank Associates Class

Tellers, customer service representatives (CSRs), receptionists, and even bank guards can learn how investment programs benefit customers (by providing better service), the bank (by increasing fee income), and employees themselves (through incentives for referrals). The emphasis in these sessions is on attracting funds for investments from outside the bank's own deposit base. Any lingering concerns usually disappear when the bank employees learn simple, direct methods of how and when to make a referral.

Leaping the Cultural Barrier

Experience has proven that the most effective solutions for overcoming remaining cultural differences between bankers and investment representatives begin with education programs. A series of carefully planned and executed courses covering the gamut of investments, strategies, and benefits of cooperative teamwork is essential—if banks don't have this they won't have an exceptional program. The contrasts between the banking environment and the representative's method of achieving objectives are recognized as opportunities to manage the combined business in the most productive manner.

Bank executives are rightfully wary of seating high-pressure, sell-like-there's-no-tomorrow sales people in their lobbies. Bankers must feel comfortable that revenue generation from needs-based investment transactions need not conflict with the traditional banking environment. One way to assure this is for the representative to conduct a sales "interview" with a bank executive, demonstrating how they get to know the customer's needs, life cycle, and risk tolerance. They show that they have been taught not just to close a sale today but to develop a relationship for the next 10 years. The philosophy is focused on building relationships and doing long-term business.

When evaluating a third-party marketer, banks need to look closely at the philosophy underlying the potential partner's educational system. Appreciating the concept of conservative, needs-based selling is vital for banks getting into brokerage because they are being much more closely audited and examined as to how they provide these services. Banks must maintain extremely high standards. So bankers better be very conscientious about teaching representatives and their colleagues how to conduct themselves.

Developing a "Referral Machine"

Using proven methods to increase cooperation and trust and demonstrating how investment programs can complement bank products and enhance customer relationships assures the success of the program.

To be successful, representatives must realize they are continuously and simultaneously selling to two different constituencies: bank customers and the bankers they work with.

Nothing works as well as personal experience with a service, though many representatives have learned that a good way to achieve buy-in is to do a thorough financial plan for bank managers and other colleagues.

The best representatives will continuously "sell" themselves to their bank colleagues by explaining investment products and their benefits to the bank and the customer. They invite branch members to be part of informational seminars for customers which in turn helps the managers to understand the value of the services being offered. They are actively involved in every branch meeting, communicate continuously with branch staff, and nurture a "referral machine" flowing in two directions.

An extremely effective way investment representatives can continue to break down cultural walls is to generate referrals for bank products. Investment representatives should understand one of their primary aims is to help the bank, and the most tangible sign of success comes as representatives set and achieve specific cross-referral goals. An action plan with specific goals for referrals back to the bank demonstrates commitment and increases essential communication with bank managers. Everyone should agree to a value statement reflecting this cooperation and to understand how referrals are generated. At the most sophisticated level, continuing bank associate education programs address these topics by educating nonregistered bankers on securities or other alternative investment possibilities and the different ways to analyze a customer's situation through financial planning.

One initiative enables managers and representatives to conduct this education on-site at the institution. Another bank associate initiative works with top management. For example, at one Midwest holding company that controls a number of banks, the heads of those banks have gathered to discuss investment program philosophy and how to better integrate their management process.

The Talent Pool

Where is the talent coming from to staff bank investment programs? A major source is the traditional Wall Street brokerage. Why would a broker leave a wirehouse and join a bank? It has certainly become a common occurrence. As brokerage business moves away from wirehouses and into banks, there has been somewhat of a broker exodus. Some of these people seem to have decided they want out of a big city, big company environment and would like to work in smaller banks in communities offering a more inviting lifestyle.

Banks offer distinct advantages. First of all, there's walk-in traffic, which is almost unheard of in a wirehouse, where a high percentage of transactions are handled by phone. The broker and customer seldom lay eyes on each other. In addition, representatives have a built-in referral system with bank tellers and CSRs. The average customer has three CDs at three other banks. If they like a representative's ideas they will liquidate a CD from another bank to buy packaged investment products.

Many bank-based brokers gain access to mortgage loan applications (with customer permission), which obviously are unavailable to wire house brokers. It is a road map to success because everything the customer has or owns should be on the mortgage loan application.

More important, bank brokers start with customer trust. The media has done a wonderful job of convincing people that Wall Street brokers are a bunch of scoundrels. They aren't, of course, but when wire house representatives start working in a bank and find that people smile at them, it makes an impact. These brokers aren't any smarter in banks today than they were on Wall Street yesterday. They just changed venues and have been well educated.

A Sales System That Works

Education is not a one-time event, particularly for brokers who have entered the bank environment from wire houses and need help in learning a new selling method. The best way we know to educate bank brokers in sales techniques is the Pro Plus System, a proprietary program developed for *INVEST* by a company known as Top Producer. It's an integrated method based on the actual experiences of top sales people which converts their activities into a working formula that is put into practice every day. Pro Plus provides experiences specific to an individual representative in a bank but useful to all others.

Phil Broyles, the designer of Pro Plus, is the leading authority on sales representative productivity in the world. He counts most of the major brokerage firms in the industry among his clients and has taught over 30,000 representatives how to be more productive.

Broyles is a great communicator. His energy level is always intense, but he has fun. He captures your attention. When he built an exclusive program to teach financial representatives how to be successful selling in a banking environment, he studied the business and learned how bank representatives differ from Wall Street brokers. The resulting Pro Plus System creates certain daily behaviors in sales representatives that are known to make them successful.

Participating representatives receive a complete program at the start, and then a monthly cassette tape and printed bulletin which highlight the successes of representatives applying the system. The combination of the bulletin and the tape works well because some of us respond better to auditory than visual stimulation. Studies reveal that about half of the representatives read the bulletin, half listen to the tape, and 85 percent of them listen to it in their car on the way to work. Since the company started using Pro Plus, average representative productivity has jumped by 60 percent.

Whether a bank builds or buys its brokerage, it needs an education program like this for its representatives to be successful. They have to be taught how to be successful. They need certain natural skills, an extroverted personality and the ability to communicate both on paper and verbally. And they must be smart enough to pass the legal examinations to demonstrate they know what they are selling.

But even top-notch communication skills won't make them successful unless they have certain work habits. Work habits are taught, not something we wake up with one morning. Practice is good as long as the right things are practiced. Practicing a mistake over and over just reinforces the mistake.

The 10 Commandments are the embodiment of the Pro Plus Sales System (Exhibit 5-1). One underlying theme jumps off the page: Self-motivation. Representatives may have the energy and the desire but they're stuck in neutral if they don't know how to structure it. Pro Plus and its 10 Commandments provide structure. Representatives set goals and action plans and review them twice daily. They do a specific number of qualified referrals each week. Without structure, it's too easy to say, "Oh, I'll do it tomorrow." Successful representatives are disciplined. They do the same things, the right things, over and over

Exhibit 5-1 *INVEST* Pro Plus 10 Commandments

1. Review goals/action plans twice daily.
2. Generate 30+ qualified referrals/leads each week.
3. Conduct 15+ sales interviews each week.
4. Ask "11 Quick Questions" to identify problems and needs.
5. Focus on 3 products each month: present them successfully.
6. Write 5+ orders each week: $1,000+ average commission per order.
7. Follow-up 6 times with Prospects-In-Progress (PIPs).
8. Contact 10 of your top 100 A-book clients each week for follow-up business.
9. Conduct 1+ seminar every two months.
10. Generate 4+ financial plans each month.

© MCMXCII Top Producer

again. A very successful representative may set goals as high as 60 qualified referrals and 30 sales interviews—and meet them.

INVEST University

There are numerous systems for educating bank employees and representatives, including intensive courses conducted at the home office of the third-party marketer, tutorials provided by independent educational consultants, and the "university" concept utilized by brokerage and investment companies. Our firm decided to take the university concept one step further. The *INVEST* University student body comes from both our own employees and those of our subscriber banks. Its underlying concept is that all educational elements need to be coordinated to be most effective, employees thrive when they have a well-defined developmental pathway, and that everyone responds well to recognition for completion of any difficult assignment, including course work.

The investment business has become much more complicated in the years since banks simply offered their customers a few mutual funds. Today, representatives need in-depth skills in financial planning, pension services, and a wide variety of product categories, ever-changing regulatory issues and selling techniques. At the heart of the *INVEST* University idea was an understanding that a coordinated and integrated program of instruction in all of these areas was needed for everyone involved in the distribution of investment products.

In addition to continuous education on the fundamentals of the business, representatives and bank employees need to develop new skills and techniques to cope with the changing and increasing number of services in their portfolios.

INVEST University offers intensive course work and a rigorous testing process. In part this is designed to satisfy requirements anticipated from NASD and other regulatory agencies. Another unique feature of the school is its willingness to coordinate additional course work with outside sources to encourage continuous development.

Under an academic scholarship program, there is no cost to the subscribing bank for enrollment of its personnel at *INVEST* University (except for travel and related expenses).

To sum up, with all the new firms entering the third-party marketing business in recent years, banks should be sure to check their credentials in educating representatives and employees of the bank on an ongoing basis. Since representative satisfaction and effectiveness is directly linked to the quality and degree to which they are educated, visit the education facilities and review all modules of instruction and how they are presented. Skimping on the education of representatives can be very, very costly for the bank and its reputation.

CHAPTER 6

Financial Planning— Leveraging Customer Trust

Over the years, bank marketers have used a vast array of techniques to encourage customers to consolidate more of their savings and investing dollars within one institution. They have achieved only limited success, in large part because they have not been able to convince the customer to reveal where additional assets are located.

Many bankers have found financial planning services provide their most valuable tool to uncover assets held outside the bank while providing a real customer service by helping their clients to invest strategically. Banks have the inside track on financial planning because wirehouses and insurance companies have strong brands and high quality sales staffs but do not enjoy deep customer trust. Banks have brand-name recognition and customers with a need walking in the door, and adding financial planning to the existing array of services creates a win/win situation.

While bankers realize their clients have assets with other banks and investment companies, most would be shocked to learn how little of their clients' assets they currently control. A study of financial planning clients revealed they have 10 times more total amount of investable assets than they would typically disclose to their bank through a transaction-only relationship. The study compared investable assets disclosed by 5,991 financial planning client households between January 1, 1991, and December 31, 1992, with those revealed by transaction-only clients. Bank clients utilizing financial planning services disclose an average of $361,000 in investable assets (excluding residence and personal effects).

A further review of 1,795 financial planning cases conducted between July 1, 1992, and December 31, 1992, found over 80 percent of client assets were from outside sources, meaning these banks controlled less than 20 percent of their clients' assets. This finding contradicts long held concerns of disintermediation.

With more assets disclosed through financial planning, the primary benefit to the bank is obvious. In fact, the study found an eight-fold increase in fee income generated by invested financial planning accounts over fee income generated by transaction-only accounts. Because financial planning clients invest more over time than do transaction-only clients, the ongoing benefits are also apparent.

Many banks have trust services but most people are not trust customers. There are people with lots of money who could be trust customers but the banks haven't recognized them yet, either because they never identify their assets or because the customers haven't sought out trust services. There is a real potential for banks with trust departments if they would offer financial planning services to more customers. Bankers will find new trust customers not previously identified because they aren't taking out mortgages or other loans. Their debt is paid off. How do bankers find out where this money is? The most effective way we know is through financial planning.

Plan to Plan

The market opportunity for financial planning is still wide open. We estimate that fewer than 10 percent of American households have actually had a plan done for them. And yet 79 percent of people in the baby boomer generation say they want and need financial planning services. A study conducted by Gallup for *American Banker* indicated 38 percent of people with accounts at financial institutions were interested in obtaining financial planning from a bank (Exhibit 6-1).

Client demand for financial planning services in banks is on the rise. *INVEST* has seen demand for free financial planning services climb by 300 percent in just two years. Banks are an obvious solution, because customers trust them.

Institutions which have embraced the financial planning process have achieved remarkable results. One example is Liberty Bank in Middletown, CT, which experienced an 83 percent jump in fee income

Exhibit 6-1 Open Minds: Consumers Look at Nontraditional Services

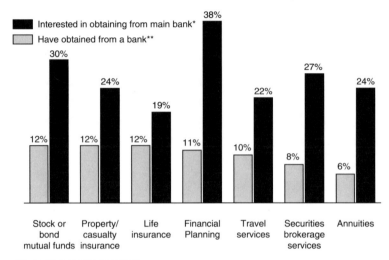

*Percentage of all respondents
**People who designate commercial bank as main institution

Source: *American Banker*/Gallup 1993 Consumer Survey.
© *American Banker.* Reprinted with permission.

from its investment services program within a six-month period after initiating a bank-wide financial planning campaign.

Planning services lend credibility to the bank's investment program and help build relationships not only with bank clients but also with bank personnel and management. By providing financial planning, investment representatives are perceived as professional, caring providers of a valuable service; this helps with referral generation.

Doing what is best for the customer involves solving short-term needs and offering long-term strategies. Banks benefit when they build stronger client relationships. In an environment of diminishing customer loyalty to brands and institutions of all types, customer retention is a vital concern and financial planning provides the key to building a long lasting attachment.

Financial planning is a defensive as well as an offensive tool. If the bank down the street already offers planning, competing banks need it just to keep up. If the competition doesn't offer it, it's a great service edge for attracting new business.

Banks must let customers know right up front there isn't any catch to financial planning. If banks offer planning services at no cost, they must advise customers that while there is no fee for the plan itself, if the customer takes some action there may be fees on the products they purchase. It should be emphasized that the customer does not have to buy or invest in anything, although most do take some action.

More Important Now Than Ever

As previously noted, the primary motivation for banks entering the investment products business has been defensive—as CDs bought in the 1980s matured, "sticker shock" caused customers to look for investments with more income. Retirees in particular have faced tough decisions, particularly those who were exchanging a $100,000 CD yielding 10 percent for the same product today yielding only 3 percent or less a year. Even the most thoughtful retirement programs have been impoverished if they were based solely on interest rate products.

Younger people are beginning to realize that doing what their parents did isn't going to get them through retirement. The days when most people worked 25 years for the same company and retired with a "fat" pension are gone. Today, people are likely to live 25 years or more after retirement and they must prepare. Many are just beginning to appreciate the effect on finances of living longer. The fear of dying has been replaced by the fear of outliving retirement assets. And, it is becoming more apparent that younger generations may not collect the generous Social Security paid today. Banks have an opportunity and responsibility to help people solve these dilemmas.

The concept of financial planning is relatively new for most people. It hasn't been available to the average customer until recently, nor did most people think they needed it. Banks still have a tremendous opportunity to help people in their fifties and sixties to reposition assets, many of whom will live longer lives that will last well into their eighties and nineties. Younger retirees are often desperate for help. And there are huge waves of people in their forties and early fifties right behind them. Fifteen years ago these baby boomers, representing the largest segment of the U.S. population, were tying up tennis courts from coast to coast. Today, their kids are through college, they are playing golf and starting to think about how they will survive retirement. Early on in their life cycles their money was tied up in establishing themselves; now it's needed for investment in their future, and they want help in this redeployment.

Modular Planning

One problem with financial planning until recently is that most plans tried to solve all the client's problems at one time. A comprehensive plan contained so much information for the client to digest, it usually went on the shelf with little or no action being taken. Today, modular plans which are broken down into bite-sized pieces to solve a particular need are proving to be much more effective. They address concerns such as retirement or college funding, estate planning, lump sum distribution, and portfolio allocation very closely tied to a client's financial life cycle. Their single priority focus keeps the client, as well as the representative, on track for achieving what's important today. And because there is a greater chance the plan will be implemented successfully, there's a much better possibility the customer will return for a new plan when the next phase in a life cycle comes along.

Most people have a portfolio they've put together over a number of years, a hodge podge with no clear direction. Bank representatives should sit down with them and see whether they have done the right job for themselves. In doing so, the representative finds out where the customer wants to go and can provide a road map to get there. After clients receive their targeted financial plan, a vast majority will take some action right away. As time goes on, they will evolve into following the whole plan. In addition to selling nontraditional products, the representative can use the plan to illustrate how traditional bank products—

when combined with investment products—help the client achieve goals.

The representative should understand that completing a professional plan takes some time, often a week or two. The temptation to sell a prospect some kind of investment product on the spot must be tempered, but the payoff is well worth it. Once clients understand the importance of a plan—and they usually do as soon as the problems and opportunities are pointed out—then the value of the specific product recommendations soars.

Over time, customers find that many factors can affect their financial plan including personal lifestyle changes such as children in college and moving from a large house to a small condo or market factors such as a change in interest rates. Because a financial plan focuses on customer needs, it allows for a review of the customer's objectives on a regular basis to help reposition investments to fit changing needs.

The financial plan review process is also an excellent opportunity to extend the selling curve. A successful financial planning program almost always means the representative has done a good job for the client, and therefore the most successful representatives are never afraid to ask a client for a recommendation to friends. It's a fact that over 80 percent of all clients say they are willing to give referrals, but only 10 percent have ever been asked.

Hesitation and Reluctance

Some banks are still reluctant to include financial planning on their product menus. Sound logic and experience are available to convince those who have not yet begun the process. The principal value is that the financial planning process helps banks overcome their number one problem, disintermediation of customers rather than funds.

The funds will flow anyway and people will seek other alternatives for placing them, so bankers have to come to the realization they must focus on maintaining a relationship with the customer. It has been demonstrated over and over again that people have investments in more than one bank or financial institution, and financial planning is the best available tool to smoke out these funds.

Some investment product representatives have found a virtually foolproof way to help bank managers who have not yet seen the wisdom of incorporating financial planning as a vital part of their service to customers: they simply give a free sample to senior executives and branch managers. Once these leaders see the value of the plans in their own lives, they are more likely to provide and encourage a professional planning service for their customers. If it is encouraged by senior management, financial planning can really take hold in a bank.

In addition to personal financial planning, representatives can break down cultural barriers between traditional banking and investment products by inviting branch officers to take part in financial planning seminars held for customers. It can be a real eye opener for the banker to see personally how customers express their long-term needs and concerns in words which are often quite different from those they use with bankers.

Making financial planning a cornerstone of the selling programs at banks will create a win/win/win situation:

- Financial planning will build a long-term relationship with the customer by focusing on needs, not on selling products, because the outcome of a well-executed plan is objective, not transaction-oriented.
- Financial planning is an objective tool to open the customer's eyes to the value of a variety of products including annuities as a means of providing for partial liquidity, retirement income, and estate enhancement.
- The representative will build a stronger relationship between the customer and the bank by making cross referrals to other traditional bank products. Cross-referral ratios always increase in a sales-oriented banking environment.
- Financial planning builds the representative's image as a financial consultant serving long-term customer needs with a documented plan of action, rather than an over eager broker looking for a sale today.
- The questions asked during the financial planning process give a much clearer picture of each customer's assets and, in effect, uncover hidden

assets which may come under the bank's control after a plan has been completed.
- The representative—and the bank—will definitely earn more money because the financial plan invariably uncovers far more investable assets than the customer would ordinarily reveal—most of them held outside the bank itself.

The Professional Touch

Only when we know the client by completing a financial plan are we qualified to have an opinion as to what is best for the person. That's when the sales process begins.

Customers trust bank representatives initially because they sit in the bank's lobby. The next phase in selling is to confidently tell the client what to do to implement the plan. Bank customers are often insecure. They have been bombarded with information from *Money* and *The Wall Street Journal* and *Barron's* and dozens of radio shows, television advice programs, and other sources. It's overwhelming. They want someone to sit down and say, "This is what you should do."

Taking Trust on the Road

Technology and changing lifestyles are increasing the frequency of customer meetings held in the home. It was with this in mind that *INVEST* developed a software program that runs on laptop or desktop computers called The Financial Horizons Toolkit[SM]. It's a proprietary computerized financial planning service that lets bank customers review options instantaneously for diversifying an investment portfolio, initiating systematic savings for purchase of a home or to build a nest egg, planning for retirement, building a college education fund, or reducing current income taxes on investments.

Tools such as this are intended to provide representatives with an easy-to-use "point-of-sale" system to help clients plan for current and future financial goals. Answers to questions regarding risk tolerance, specific needs for retirement income or college tuition, tax issues, and how to handle a lump sum distribution are displayed quickly in a clear format. Various investment scenarios can be created to show how different investment products will help reach highly personalized needs.

The system was also designed to help customers invest cash on hand after the customer goes through a modified financial planning process. Longer term, a certified financial planner or a chartered financial consultant should work on a formal plan, but the portable program is an immediate, interactive tool which allows clients to participate, hands-on.

A bank contemplating a similar program needs to take certain legal steps in addition to building a very sophisticated software application. A compliance disclaimer must be shown before the client proceeds through any financial planning illustrations. The client should be offered a menu from which to choose modular plans for various needs such as retirement savings, and college funding projections or handling a pension plan distribution. Often after a customer goes through one element of a computerized financial planning service, it turns them on to detailed financial planning.

Whether they generate a full-fledged financial plan or a proposal generated by a portable system like The Financial Horizons Toolkit, successful representatives report over 75 percent of the recommendations made in these plans are actually acted upon. Clients follow the representative's advice because they want the guidance.

Marketing Pensions through Bank Brokerage

Bank trust departments have traditionally serviced the business clients of their financial institution and maintained a substantial market share of retirement plan assets. However, many banks have pension prospects who are not typical trust customers either due to the asset size of their plan or their preference to not pay trustee fees. This market is an ideal target for a bank's brokerage division or their third-party marketing firm.

Determining how to structure pension services to service this market is crucial to its success. Pension services normally offered include:

- a proposal service to evaluate the appropriate type of pension plan for the business;
- the availability of prototype plans to assist clients in setting up a plan and trust;

- plan administration services to provide employee and IRS reporting services;
- investment flexibility to allow for adequate diversification under ERISA rules; and
- ongoing technical expertise to consult with clients regarding the tax and legal issues that affect qualified retirement plans.

Although no program should attempt to provide tax or legal advice or specifically do every function itself, having an alliance with firms that can provide these services is essential.

Bankers have four options for providing full-service pension planning through a bank brokerage system: build it from scratch, buy a pension package, leverage through mutual fund programs, or leverage through a third-party marketing firm.

Attempting to build a pension sales and marketing program from scratch can be a costly undertaking involving many expenses including labor costs to hire people with pension expertise, plan document costs to purchase a prototype plan program, and computer costs to purchase the hardware and software to do pension proposals or administration.

Buying the whole pension package of prototype plans from third-party firms can still leave possible holes in service to do pension proposals, plan administration, or to hire staff with the expertise to talk to clients.

Investment companies often provide pension services to banks; however, the client is usually restricted to investing in those companies' mutual funds. Diversification into bank CDs or other individual securities is not possible. This approach generally does not include plan administration and IRS filings so the bank and, ultimately, the client ends up having to fend for themselves for these services.

The other alternative available to banks is to obtain these pension services through a third-party marketing brokerage firm which offers maximum flexibility with investments and plan administration. The best third-party firms offer complete pension services that include a prototype plan document that permits packaged products, annuities, insurance, UITs, and individual securities as well as bank products so that the clients can easily meet their fiduciary responsibilities for portfolio diversification under one plan.

When evaluating any of these options, bankers should carefully consider costs to the client who are not used to paying fees for services. Fees that may be incurred can include plan document fees, plan document amendment fees, account set-up fees, annual investment account fees, distribution fees on withdrawals, plan administration set-up fees, annual administration fees, distribution calculation and processing fees, loan administration fees, fees to prepare 1099R tax reporting forms, and termination fees for transferring the plan to another company. The best third-party firms often eliminate these fees and price plan administration services at wholesale prices.

Support services such as pension training and marketing materials are also an important consideration when deciding which option to choose. The best programs offer marketing materials that include seminars, brochures, advertising slicks, sample prospecting letters, and lists of business owner prospects that can be tapped in areas around a bank's branches.

Banks that market pension services to corporate customers open doors for long-term client relationships. The potential opportunities to provide additional products and services to business customers is limited only by a bank's offerings and can include business checking, direct deposit, and commercial lending services. In addition to pension plans, personal financial planning services can be offered as a perk to key employees or the entire group of employees.

Pension plans are exceptionally profitable for banks. Net commission revenues to the bank are substantially more for pension accounts than for the average retail account. Simplified Employee Pension (SEP) plans generate more than two and one-half times a retail account, and corporate pension accounts, such as profit sharing, money purchase or 401(k) plans generate over seven times more commission than does the average retail account.

Do It Right

Whether as part of the retail investment products offering or the pension services of a bank, any institution using financial planning must make sure to do it right. A poorly executed planning service, or one which does not have careful controls, can backfire and create customer ill will or even legal problems.

It is important for the bank to utilize the services of a *strong, independent and highly qualified* financial services organization to implement the plan. Brokerage representatives should not try to do a comprehensive plan alone because a good program demands sophisticated methods of evaluating and solving personal goals and objectives. Remember, the window of opportunity may never be wider for establishing long-term relationships through financial planning.

CHAPTER 7

Integration of the Investment Program

To survive in today's increasingly competitive financial services market, banks have changed some of the fundamental aspects of their culture—particularly when it comes to making nontraditional products such as mutual funds, annuities, and life insurance available.

Banks that have been the most successful, regardless of size, have done so by integrating investment products as a mainstream, core business of the institution. Getting everybody in the bank familiar with and enthusiastic about these products has been the real challenge.

How can banks persuade the tellers, customer service representatives, and branch managers to care about the sale of mutual funds or annuities which may be a mystery to them in the first place? How do banks provide incentive for these products to managers who have been compensated primarily on the basis of how many deposits they attracted? Banks must motivate their people through incentives.

The first step should be for the chief executive officer of the bank to make it clear the institution is committed to succeed in the fee income business and to deliver alternative products to customers. There should be no question about whether this is an experiment or is in some way secondary to other retail bank activities. Getting commitment in the lobby is critical.

While investment sales programs have proliferated, few banks have instituted a truly integrated sales culture. Some bankers adopt a sales program or launch periodic promotions to increase sales of specific products and sincerely believe they have put a sales culture in place. But ongoing commitment and tangible rewards are too often missing and the programs do not reach their full potential.

Integration relies on making the delivery of alternative products a stated goal of the bank, but to assure that everyone embraces this notion, these products should become one of the things by which employees are measured. Integration happens after everyone senses the resolve of senior management, and there are few better ways of demonstrating this than to tie the products into incentive payments and performance reviews.

How does a bank go about this sometimes daunting task? Fortunately, nowadays the first mention of the word "sales" to bankers elicits interest in learning new techniques. In the past this wasn't always true;

selling was alien to the culture of most banks. Today, however, bankers realize they are in the sales and service business and this means thou shalt approach the customer to sell.

Increasingly, bankers have found fee income programs can change their institutions by helping them to adopt a sales culture and demonstrating how effective sales can generate income for the bank's bottom line.

How One Bank Did It

After years of making alternative investments available through its standard program with full-time registered Series 7 representatives, California Federal Bank's senior management decided in late 1988 to integrate its sales program throughout the bank by switching to a fully integrated platform program.

Cal Fed made a concerted effort through its subsidiary, Cal Fed Investment Services, to license over 600 employees—including managers—at its 126 branch offices. These individuals were then educated to sell insurance and annuity products developed specifically for platform personnel to offer to their customers. Current Series 7 representatives' roles and responsibilities shifted so they served as internal wholesalers for the program. Within the first 12 months, the program produced in excess of $200 million in annuity sales.

Needless to say, this $200 million got the attention of the bank's senior management. In 1989, the annuities sales effort was about the biggest thing happening at Cal Fed. Following the initial success, Cal Fed's senior management decided to incorporate selling techniques into the entire retail bank, starting by establishing aggressive goals for branch managers for fee income as well as for traditional bank products. Contests were developed involving the daily measurement of sales production, and senior management responded to the branches on both good and poor performance.

In early 1990, management saw an opportunity to make these employees even more productive. Since they had already trained and licensed their branch staff to sell alternative investment products, they decided to register certain employees to become Series 6 representatives, giving them the ability to offer alternative investments as well as offering bank products. In 1991, Cal Fed did $300 million in mutual fund business alone. Because of its success, Cal Fed became a model for other banks across the country wanting to set up platform programs.

Cal Fed is a classic example of a successful integration program. The bank has manager compensation plans and incentives in place. It adjusted job descriptions for everyone. The result is that the average Cal Fed representative produces nearly twice as much gross commissions per month compared with the average representative in typical programs across the country. Everyone benefits from this production. It works when banks do it the right way.

One of the true values of a platform program is accomplishing a level of integration within the bank's culture which couldn't be achieved in any other way.

Commitment Starts at the Top

Developing and integrating a sales culture is an ongoing process requiring top management's unwavering commitment. This commitment translates into letting bank employees know the fee income program is important to the bank and investment representatives, tellers, and service personnel who must all work together.

Top bank executives must be willing to transform compensation packages and make other fundamental adjustments to ingrain fee income programs into the core strategy of the bank. Otherwise, these nontraditional programs will most likely fail to reach their potential, resulting in loss of fee income, lower profits, and inferior service to the bank's customers.

At the start, senior executives should understand the cultural shift involved in hiring and integrating sales representatives who are paid on a commission basis. This hurdle can be critical, since many senior bank officers are mistrustful of a system in which employees rely almost exclusively on commissions for their income. There's a sense they will be too aggressive and will frighten conservative bank customers. Once bank officers accept the concept that the bank's goals can be achieved if some employees receive incentive compensation for achieving their goals, they find having commission sales personnel in the branches for delivering fee income products is not threatening.

Apart from the compensation issues, senior bank officers often make two kinds of mistakes when establishing investment programs in their lobbies. The first is to take the "benign neglect" approach, in effect saying, "Well, I'm not sure we should even be in this business at all but I'll give it a try. Put the representatives out in the lobby and leave them alone. Let the program run on its own steam and see how these guys do. If they're successful, we'll keep it around; if they fail then we haven't lost much." In the second approach, CEOs are victims of their own enthusiasm, overmanaging the program and trying to transfer its sales and marketing concepts too quickly into other sectors of the bank.

The most successful programs are those in which senior managers have taken a number of steps that are very similar, all of which require some fundamental rethinking and willingness to change more than just the cosmetics. The first step is to gradually make sales a part of everyone's responsibilities by changing job descriptions and titles throughout the bank. These descriptions should reflect the bank's evolving emphasis toward sales. New job descriptions will also bring new job titles into play. In some banks, branch managers have become sales managers and platform employees become sales associates. Job descriptions include a requirement for employees to make referrals when they come across a customer who should be talking to the investment center.

To support its growing emphasis on sales, Mid-America Federal Savings Bank not only looked at current positions but also restructured its hiring process to insure all new employees understood the importance of their position's sales responsibilities. The

Integration of the Investment Program 121

bank has given attitude and aptitude toward sales more weight than skill at a particular task on the theory that skills can be taught but the other attributes are inborn.

Achieving a true sales culture means difficult emotional decisions for many people in the bank. Good sales demand recurring education, incentives and rewards, concepts sometimes foreign to bank personnel. Some of the best programs have embraced the hoopla and excitement associated with sales contests and glitzy awards ceremonies. Recognition is contagious, events addictive. Banks should be truly proud of their sales contest winners.

Performance review criteria for every retail employee—from managers to customer service representatives to tellers—should include a requirement for appropriate cooperation or participation in the nontraditional banking program. Obviously, the degree of participation is governed by regulations, training, and access to information. However, the bank employee must sense that the investment program is critical to the success of the bank, and employees will be measured by how much they contribute to this success.

Additional compensation is an option to help motivate staff to participate more fully and directly. In most cases, the prospect of extra dollars in a paycheck is a strong motivator. Even without a formal incentive compensation program for platform staff, support for the investment program must be included in job descriptions and performance expectations. While merely changing job titles and descriptions cannot change the bank's culture, it is an important first step in helping all bank employees understand the importance of sales to the bank's success.

Motivation at the Branch Level

Unless the branch manager is fully behind the investment program in his or her facility, it will not work. The brokerage representative will feel like Cinderella and will be treated as an outcast by the retail bank staff. The easiest way to assure that this never happens is to include successful implementation of the investment products program into the branch manager's annual performance review and compensation. If the program meets or exceeds its goals, the manager should benefit with a defined and meaningful bonus.

If the program does not meet goals, the manager should see a reduction in incentive compensation. Clearly, the bank senior management needs to have sensible expectations and needs to set achievable goals for the branch managers. A realistic forecast of fee income potential for each branch and the steps necessary to reach it can be obtained by using a tested projection model for predicting fee income and following expert advice to get the program running.

Bankers should keep the goals for managers short term, even measuring performance on a quarterly basis. That keeps managers focused on the program because their rewards are received quicker. But the key thing is to emphasize profitability, which means senior management must make goals achievable but still be something branch managers have to stretch for.

Another option is to give the entire branch staff opportunities to enhance personal income if they meet goals for success in the investment products program. Money is a powerful motivator, and a compensation plan says: "Fee income matters. It matters as much as anything else you do in the bank, and we are willing to pay to achieve it." If generation of fee income from alternative products does not have equal weight with other traditional banking goals then it is not likely to achieve its potential.

Some banks give everyone in the branch specific sales goals—for example, not only for the number of referrals to a fee income program but also for opening CD accounts. In these cases, the importance of compensating every employee supporting the fee income program is obvious. When everyone in the branch pulls in the same direction for the same things, miraculous things can happen.

MidAmerica saw real cultural integration occur in 1993, when a new branch performance incentive program was implemented. The new program provided bonuses to everyone from branch managers to tellers. Ultimately, the bank seeks to develop its branches into profit centers and pay bonuses based on the branch's performance.

If the integration process is successful in a bank, the only visible line between deposits and fee income will be the requirement to make sure customers understand clearly that investment products are not the same as insured deposits. Disclosure policies must be a part of all education efforts, of course, particularly as banks move toward full integration of fee-based services into the retail institution.

The Importance of Education

If participation in the investment program is to be included in the job description and performance measurement of employees, then senior managers should provide a comprehensive educational program for all platform people, whether they are Series 6 registered professionals or are nonregistered.

The management of Liberty Bank in Connecticut was concerned about retail bank employees who felt the investment program staff was more competition rather than part of the branch teams. But the bank president encouraged a process of education to help make integration work. Liberty's investment managers began to visit the branches, emphasizing their roles as financial planners. They made an effort to get to know branch personnel and showing them how the investment program could help their customers and the bank. It was a lengthy process, but strong support from the bank's management has contributed to the success of the program.

One of the things Liberty and other banks have found is that employees want a better understanding of their product lines. The most popular on-site education programs are those which provide basic information about investment products to tellers, customer service representatives, and other platform personnel. This education empowers the employee with information about how valuable these services are to customers, to the bank, and to themselves. Education of tellers and platform staff can also help avoid the pitfalls of inappropriate referrals by nonqualified people.

Instruction can work both ways, however, and investment representatives must also know what is going on in the bank, be knowledgeable about products, and be prepared to cross-refer when possible. Top bank management needs to foster this exchange to achieve complete integration.

A variety of easy-to-grasp techniques can help tellers build a bank's investment products business. Simply keeping an eye on the maker of checks is one device. If tellers see a customer is routinely depositing checks from a brokerage house, that person is probably an investor and a candidate for financial planning services. Other sure signs of potential investment products customers include people with trust accounts, small business owners, and the biggest category of all, people with maturing CDs. Branch personnel should see these people as opportunities to offer multiple products and services not just a CD renewal. To reinforce this concept, MidAmerica implemented an aggressive funds retention program. If the customer renews a CD or invests the money in a nontraditional product through the bank, the transaction counts toward the branch's performance goals.

The on-site education of tellers, customer service representatives, receptionists, and even bank guards also helps to dispel misconceptions about the sales process. These employees are shown how the investment program benefits everyone: the customers, by providing better service; the bank, by increasing fee income; and the associates themselves, through incentives for referrals.

Too often, fee-based programs are so geared toward in bound referrals they leave other bank departments out of the loop. New account worksheets in the investment products business should include a section of questions which ask what other services bank customers currently use or need. This information is then given to the branch manager for further follow-up.

Customer service representatives in the bank are much more willing to make referrals for financial planning than for a specific product. Telling a customer to buy a mutual fund from the representative might entail assuming a performance risk which makes a CSR uncomfortable. But, the CSR is often more willing to send a client to have a strategic plan completed.

The benefits of encouraging a sales culture throughout the bank are significant. By limiting the "sales mentality" strictly to the fee income program, the bank misses out on an opportunity to increase customer relationships and the potential for greater customer retention. As the integration of fee income has evolved, managements are realizing the importance of commissioned sales representatives for other products, from loans to home equity and from credit cards to safe deposit boxes.

A good third-party firm will help bankers understand how to integrate traditional and nontraditional products into one sales culture which meshes with the historical image of the bank. Steps include breaking down deposit and investment fee income goals into

Integration of the Investment Program

quarterly, monthly, weekly, or daily segments. A process for managing the goal setting and achievement is put in place. Bonus payment procedures are established. Specific steps to attain integration are mandated, such as sharing of customer information between the retail bank and the investment products manager.

Other techniques include offering a complimentary financial plan for every mortgage loan application. The bank CEO from time to time can send personal letters to the bank's best customers, introducing financial planning services. The bank's marketing materials can be coordinated with those of the third-party broker/dealer, expanding the scope of both.

The benefits of integration are obvious, but the real need for it is an imperative. We live in a world of commercial market share. Brokerage firms look like banks and banks feel they have to look like brokerage firms. Insurance companies look like brokerage firms, financial planning firms, and banks. Auto dealers and retirement associations offer credit cards. Credit unions are in all these businesses. Everyone is competing for the same customers. Bankers need to serve as many of their customer's needs as possible and still keep deposits in their institutions. Banks that have lost market share have found it is terribly hard and expensive to gain it back.

By instituting a truly integrated sales culture, banks can provide their customers with the variety of products and services in an environment of trust and high level of service. The customers win because they now have access to a full range of deposit and investment products at a convenient location; the banks win because they retain these customers within the bank and generate fee income. It's an ideal win/win situation.

CHAPTER 8

Brokerage in Community Banks

Over half of all commercial banks and thrifts in the United States now sell investment products. The remainder are mostly smaller institutions, often held back from getting in the business because they simply cannot generate the volume of business needed to pay the high fixed overhead costs of operating an investment program.

These well-capitalized institutions are integral parts of their communities. Many of their customers opened their first passbook savings account at the bank as a child and now have their first mortgage loan with the same institution. These are grassroots banks where the customers are often greeted by name as they come in the bank. There's a mutual sense of loyalty between customer and bank—both *de novo* and established institutions—that doesn't exist at less personal money center banks or at large regional institutions.

With this kind of customer base, community bankers have an opportunity and responsibility to provide every available financial product they can under their charter to meet customer needs. They don't think customers should have to go anywhere else for a financial service if the bank can possibly provide it in a way that's consistent with its reputation for quality and trust.

Most community bankers were stymied until recently when it came to offering first-class investment services. How could they provide the necessary products, due diligence, financial planning, marketing, compliance, and other intangibles such as networking with the mutual fund and insurance vendors? They needed to do many of the things a big bank does, but they didn't want to compromise on quality just because their institutions were smaller.

Prior to the 1990s, the major third-party marketers did not actively court small banks because the fixed cost of setting up support programs, which included a high level of customer service operations, was prohibitively high compared to the revenue they could generate. There just weren't enough potential customers in most of these institutions to make it meaningful for either the bank or the marketer to provide a comprehensive investment program.

One strategy third-party marketers typically have used when dealing with community banks was to strip out costly services they may have provided to medium- or larger-sized institutions. It rarely worked because community banks need these value-added services even more than the bigger banks. Education of bank staff is critical, marketing is essential, excellent clearing and recordkeeping are a must. Serious attention to all of these aspects is needed no matter how big or small the program.

Third-party marketers have developed a profitable way for community banks to participate fully in value-added programs at a fraction of what it would have cost the banks to set up these services themselves. They do so by establishing a consortium of banks, which makes it cost effective for the marketers to work with smaller institutions.

How It Works

Community banks can participate as members of a consortium which shares the cost of providing these value-added benefits. A model for these networks is the *INVEST* Community Banking Program^{SM}, in which essential functions are handled through a centralized service center with shared management which oversees all sales management and technical operations, including data input for marketing and trading purposes. From six to 15 banks can all be supported.

The network provides an extremely professional management system, a wide product lineup, and due diligence at an affordable price. The operations center is set up and staffed based upon the number of representatives housed in the consortium's banks. Generally, one sales assistant can be added for every $450,000 in gross commission produced.

The sales assistants enter all orders, do problem solving, execution, clearing, follow-up, administrative and clerical functions, and handle the customer file system for marketing and communications with clients. All the assistants are Series 6 or 7 licensed and have annuity licenses. They communicate by phone or fax with sales representatives at the member banks and are supervised by an operations manager.

From one to three registered sales representatives in each bank handle the sales process itself, adapting their techniques and styles to match the "culture" of the individual bank. These representatives have just one responsibility—to produce full-time in those branches where they have been strategically placed based upon advance branch profitability projections.

A regional manager with a Securities Principal Series 24 license is responsible for these banks. The community bank gets the benefit of representatives producing commissions on a full-time basis without the bank being responsible for management. Previously, in small programs, one representative had to devote at least a portion of his or her hours to management chores. The consortium concept provides economies of scale to enable the representatives to achieve higher productivity levels.

Under this program, the third-party marketing company recruits investment representatives, although the bank has approval over who is hired. In addition, it educates both the brokerage representative and the bank's platform personnel in cross-selling techniques which make "alternative" programs a core part of the retail bank.

The added-value tools help assure the success of any investment program, but are particularly vital in a smaller bank because of competitive challenges. The banks provide the space and a welcoming culture for the brokerage representatives to perform. But all back office work, compliance issues, and the like are totally transparent to the bank.

The first such program in the nation was established in 1993 in the Greater Atlanta area with seven member banks. The institutions range in size from as low as $40 million in assets up to $250 million in assets and are located as far as 60 miles from the service center. The program achieved an average of 142 percent of pro forma commission expectations in the first six months.

Subsequent networks have enabled banks with multiple branches, geographically distanced as much as 250 or 300 miles apart, to centralize all of their representative operations out of one location. These consortiums utilize advanced technology, including laptop computers, to assure instant and accurate communications.

In these programs, the focus is directed to three simple but challenging productivity tasks: how to intercept funds that would otherwise be disintermediated from the community bank, how to uncover assets not yet known to the bank, and finally how to attract new customers through the investment program. Systems have been developed specifically to help small banks achieve these goals through employee awareness programs, formal launch meetings, one-on-one sessions with staff, and weekly sales meetings.

Just as community bank staffs must be educated, so must their customers, many of whom have 100 percent of their cash assets in the institution. Older customers often use income from these deposits to supplement retirement programs. In an exceptionally low interest rate environment, bankers accept a responsibility to help these older customers maintain their income levels with higher yields, and yet do it in a conservative, safe manner. While disintermediation may have been a factor in the bank's decision to get into the business, customer retention is usually the main motivator.

Nonetheless, the programs are attracting new customers. The program allows investment representatives to share names and profiles of new customers with the retail side of the bank for cross-selling into existing products. As the programs mature, community banks will integrate them further into the general fabric of the institutions until it then becomes just another product and service offered by these banks. As successful implementation of the investment program becomes a part of the bank manager's goals and compensation packages, the more productive they will become for the institution as a whole.

Correspondent Programs for the Smallest Banks

A second approach to community bank programs goes deeper, addressing even smaller banks, less than

$100 million in most cases. They are definitely below the guidelines of institutions with which most third-party firms would have a direct relationship. They want to be in this business and they need value-added services more so than any other bank because they are small and have few internal resources. Buying marketing, financial planning, and other services is cost prohibitive and community bank networks may not be available to them.

For years banks have utilized correspondent relationships with other institutions for credit cards and clearing checks. *INVEST* is taking the correspondent concept into a new area by setting up investment programs that link small banks with existing subscribers to its services.

The *INVEST* Correspondent Banking Program[SM] allows small banks to participate in brokerage services the same as big banks without forgoing any of the costly and sophisticated marketing, clearing, technology, education, and other tools it takes to make these programs a success. It offers institutions which already have successful programs the opportunity to expand their revenue potential by contracting with institutions just outside their own trading areas.

The larger subscribing institutions, which serve as anchor banks, establish a correspondent relationship with smaller institutions with *INVEST* as the broker/dealer of record and the smaller institution serving as a satellite distribution outlet. These locations are treated as individual investment centers and all of the value-added services offered through the anchor bank's direct relationship with the third party are available to them. The host and its correspondents share in revenues generated.

The third-party marketer has a limited role in this process, since the subscriber's program manager oversees the relationship with the correspondent bank. The system works with both a "standard" program relationship or a "managed" program in which the program staff are on the payroll of the third-party marketer. The managed program is downstreamed to enable the subscribing bank to look at the smaller institution not as a competitor but as a partner. Likewise, the downstream corresponding institution gets the full benefit of all broker/dealer services as well as full indemnity in the securities business.

The bottom line benefit for the subscribing institution in developing correspondent relationships is enhanced fee income. The larger bank effectively expands its trade area with no additional marketing or capital investment, and only incrementally more managerial activity.

There are 8,000 banks with less than $100 million in assets. Virtually all of them are candidates either for a community banking network or a correspondent relationship with a larger institution which is already benefiting from investment products.

Implementation

Since senior managers in community banks are responsible for multiple areas, they are reluctant to take on more tasks unless there is a substantial payoff or other benefit. The decision on whether a smaller bank will enter the investment products business often depends on managerial capacity. For this reason, it is critical to select a third-party marketer which has a smooth, tested and efficient implementation program with the expertise to tailor it to any size institution.

Community bankers want clear direction in setting up their programs and will expect the implementation manager to act as a consultant in making recommendations. The issues range from program design and integration to the most minute details of setting up the program.

Bankers make decisions based on the bottom line. What will we earn from this program? Will our managers be diverted from other, more profitable activities? A competent third-party marketer will help the banker understand these questions, first by providing a solid pro forma revenue projection for the bank as a whole and each of its branches. This includes a bottom-up analysis that projects how many referrals can be expected realistically from each bank employee. The marketer helps establish goals the bank and the marketer agree are achievable, and it also determines who is responsible for reaching them.

While the third-party marketer is responsible for a large number of tasks in every program, bank officers are more involved in the details if the institution has a "standard" program than under the "managed" system.

In both standard and managed programs, the process begins with recruiting. One of the biggest issues in running any business is finding quality people. A third-party firm should have an ongoing recruiting program with a full-time recruiter in place to generate a continual flow of resumes and present good candidates to be interviewed by bank managers. Programs will succeed only if the representative works well with bank customers and bank employees.

Community bankers should examine a chart of critical path tasks and appropriate timelines before starting the implementation process, and they should make sure they understand who has responsibility for completing each task. Close surveillance is required to insure no steps are overlooked. The timelines should be tracked via computer network by the third party so all parties involved can review and update assignments and due dates.

There are no longer any mysteries in how to get a program up and running in a small bank. The only time difficulties arise is if the senior management of the bank has not made a full commitment to supporting entry into the program or has not chosen a third-party marketer with a proven record and a sensitivity to the occasional obstacles along the way. Bankers can choose among well established and successful programs—managed, standard, or platform—and have a high degree of comfort that their expectations will be met.

CHAPTER 9

Compliance

Few words in the banking vocabulary carry quite the emotional power of *compliance*. For some it conjures up visions of examiners poring over documents looking for discrepancies that could derail a manager from an otherwise happy career path, result in a substantial fine, or worse. For others, however, compliance is an accepted fact of banking life, particularly in the investment area where strict adherence is an absolute requirement for success. In the investment products business, good compliance generally means more revenue.

Rules and regulations to protect the American banking consumer go back to Alexander Hamilton, who in 1789 became the first Secretary of the Treasury and two years later established the Bank of the United States (a full 13 years before losing his life in a duel with Aaron Burr). At around the same time, the Buttonwood Agreement of 1792 established the New York Stock Exchange and with it the first standards of compliance on securities sales to which all participants had to abide.

In this century, a profusion of national and state laws beginning with the Securities Act of 1933 have established the complicated framework within which banks and broker/dealers must operate. As a nationwide company providing investment services to banks, *INVEST* is touched by 148 different regulators, including federal, state and quasi-governmental agencies in insurance, banking and securities. Each organization has its own mandate and particular vision of how things should be done. Given the virtual avalanche of new rules affecting bank mutual fund and annuity sales in the past decade, it is not surprising that some are duplicating, conflicting, and in some cases illogical.

In early 1994, a small notice in the *Federal Register* announced that henceforth banks will report the dollar volume from the sale and servicing of mutual funds and annuities during the previous quarter in their Call Report income statement. "Now it's a hot activity, and everybody wants to know who's involved and what they are doing," the FDIC's Robert F. Storch told the *American Banker*.

Secrets of Self-Regulation

Yet, despite a mountain of laws, compliance in the bank investment business is very much tied into the philosophy of self-regulation. Under legal mandate, the Securities and Exchange Commission (SEC) allows the National Association of Securities Dealers, Inc. (NASD), to enforce its own Rules of Fair Practice as well as some of the SEC's securities regulations. Adding further clout to the self-policing system are the registered securities exchanges, from the New York Stock Exchange to the Pacific Stock Exchange, which also operate under the philosophy of self-regulation. The ultimate goal of all regulation is to provide customer protection by instilling high standards of broker/dealer performance and adherence to the rules.

Banking institutions which operate their own broker/dealer and the third-party marketers providing this service each have their own compliance departments which are responsible for protecting consumer interests and assuring that all state, federal, and local regulations are heeded.

In the current atmosphere of intense scrutiny and the possibility of even more exacting regulations being imposed by Congress, compliance is viewed as a shared responsibility involving all levels of management, sales, and administration in the securities industry. By the appropriate compliance department developing its own language for explaining the standards, making sure everyone involved understands them, and verifying adherence to existing compliance procedures, each subscribing institution can feel a degree of comfort when questions arise regarding issues involving customer activity.

When *INVEST* entered the banking arena in 1982, it broke new ground. The company signaled the major national regulatory bodies its intention to establish "separate and distinct" units within banks and thrifts. The company had to demonstrate that its brokerage activities included consumer protection and a method for indemnification to subscribing banks so as not to create a potential liability to the financial institutions. Further, *INVEST* had to prove it was fully equipped to provide all of the transaction execution, order entry, clearing, customer statements, confirmation support, and related functions provided by any other major brokerage. None of the federal agencies registered any opposition to the plan (their way of giving it a blessing).

Banks choosing to become subscribers of a third-party marketer inherit the compliance mantle of the service provider. A bank acquiring a broker/dealer assumes the history of the unit it purchased. Banks which start their own broker/dealers start the process from step one.

The first action for any bank considering a relationship with a third-party marketer or brokerage service should be to verify that the potential partner has a clear record with the SEC, NASD, state securities administrations, FDIC, OCC, and the Office of Thrift Supervision. A finding of no history or current action pending in the files of these organizations indicates the company has followed the rules and regulations.

Any bank—and for that matter any consumer—can check almost instantly on the current compliance status of any broker or individual registered representative. The NASD hotline for verifying if any disciplinary actions have been taken or are pending is

800/289-9999. The NASD provides a verbal report on the phone, which is followed up with a written report within five days if requested. In addition, members of the North American Securities Administrators Association (NASAA) maintain detailed records on a state-by-state basis. Any banker or private citizen can call the NASAA at 202/737-0900 for the name and number of the agency appropriate to a given state; a call to the state usually gets a response during the first phone contact.

As every banker knows, in recent years the three principal banking regulators along with NASD and the SEC have become concerned about potential confusion on the part of consumers about whether investment products are insured. In order to assure that banks are allowed to continue to sell investment products in lobbies, third-party marketers and a bank with its own broker/dealer must go to every possible length to protect consumer interests and eliminate confusion about the nature of the investment products.

Separate and distinct standards must be rigid and rigorously applied. Regulatory-tested disclosure forms that clearly state the services are distinct from the retail services of the financial institution must be used with every customer. Training and supervision of sales personnel must be disciplined and consistent. Banks should have a compliance manual for nonregistered employees, and education and training seminars should be held for employees at their headquarters and branches.

Banks are asking for trouble if their brokerage does business at a desk in the lobby under a tiny or confusing sign that doesn't differentiate it from the retail bank, or if the customer and the registered representative do not sign a disclosure statement. The essence of self-regulation is a willingness to go beyond the letter of the law and to insist that its spirit be maintained as well. Anything less will surely provoke the lawmakers into passing yet more unnecessary and burdensome regulations.

Working with Regulators

Part and parcel of self-policing by banks with broker/dealers or third-party marketers are detailed examinations by the NASD. The association requires that the activities of its member institutions and appropriately registered individuals, depending on the product offered, be supervised by a Registered Securities Principal. The broker is required to conduct an internal inspection by its own compliance examiner at least annually. If it doesn't, and the NASD finds the broker has not followed compliance with all of its rules, a disciplinary action can be brought.

As a matter of course the NASD examines brokers each year or two and, along with the SEC and state securities departments, has the authority to go into any registered branch office in its jurisdiction to satisfy itself that the branch is complying with all requirements. Brokers with no deficiencies over a period of time may be examined only every other year.

However, some states have additional requirements that are even more stringent than the SEC and NASD.

There is little point in antagonizing regulators. In fact, they can become a resource. When they visit the bank, welcome them, give them a comfortable area in which to sit and make sure all their requests for books and records are provided without delay. If any deficiencies are found, correct them immediately, ideally before the examination is complete.

To assure a clean bill of health during visits by the outside examiners, the bank, or its broker must first assure a strong self-policing system. Every bank or third-party marketer should have an automated system checking transactions. For example, *INVEST* has developed a sophisticated daily automated surveillance system which picks up transactions that fall out of specific parameters either by size or number. The compliance department then checks the account to find out why the unusual trade occurred. One compliance program checks on sales fee break points. If a transaction falls slightly below a break point, thus denying the consumer a lower sales charge, a yellow flag goes up and an inquiry is made as to the circumstances. The break point for a fund might be $100,000 to qualify for a reduced sales charge; if compliance sees a transaction of $98,000, the sales representative is asked why an additional $2,000 was not invested to give the customer the benefit of the break point. There may be a perfectly good reason, but the surveillance program is something that the representatives know is in place and it allows *INVEST* to service with confidence.

The next line of defense is compliance examiners, teams of securities industry professionals who have passed registration and qualification exams to become general securities principals. These examiners routinely visit every location within the branch system to look at records and discuss activities. The examiners carry laptop computers and by the time an examination is completed at a branch, brokers immediately know all the deficiencies and how to correct them. It used to take four weeks to get examination results to a broker, but today when an examiner leaves the branch the broker is given a preliminary grade and an open book questionnaire to complete within one day.

There is no room for sloppy recordkeeping in the way the compliance department works within a bank to oversee individual representative activities. At least once a year, the third-party firm's compliance department examines each registered branch office's customer statements, reports of transactions, customer new account records, order tickets prepared and maintained, disclosure documents signed by clients and maintained at branch, monthly records of transactions provided the marketer and so forth. Following the annual examination conducted by compliance examiners, *INVEST* sends a written report to the *INVEST* manager at each subscribing institution. Bank management is given a copy of this report to satisfy itself that the controls are in place and are being followed in all operations.

Communications Compliance

The responsibility of the compliance department starts well before the customer goes into the bank lobby. Compliance reviews, in advance, all advertising, sales literature, brochures and other marketing materials, sales letters, generic correspondence, and even telemarketing scripts. Any outgoing correspondence to clients pertaining to securities transactions must be submitted to the compliance department unless it is standardized or preapproved in nature. All correspondence relating to a specific transaction, yields or rates, and anything recommending a specific security must be submitted to the compliance department. In fact, any "creative" correspondence suggesting a specific investment, quoting prices to customers, or making other recommendations must pass through compliance before it is sent, and it must be retained for a specified period established by securities regulators.

In addition, compliance will review outside activities of brokers as a precaution against conflicts of interest. Third-party compliance officers will also oversee sales activity at subscribing institutions. There's a good reason for this: it protects the banker and the representative, because there may be misinterpretation by the customer that could land even the best intentioned employee in hot water. The best course is to let the compliance department assume responsibility.

Despite reviews of every page of correspondence and careful explanation of what the representative can and can't tell a customer, there will inevitably be some complaints. What then? Banks and third-party marketers are required by the NASD to maintain written records of all complaints and their disposition. A "complaint" shall be deemed to mean any written statement (or oral from a resident of Wisconsin) of a customer or any person acting on behalf of a customer alleging a grievance involving the activities of those persons under the control of a member of the National Association of Securities Dealers, Inc., in connection with the solicitation or execution of any transaction or the disposition of securities or funds of that customer.

Complaints must be forwarded immediately by mail or fax transmission to the Compliance Department. Upon receipt, compliance personnel will assume control of the matter and send an acknowledgement letter to the customer assuring a thorough investigation.

At no time should the representative or bank personnel either respond or attempt to resolve the matter other than to acknowledge receipt of a complaint thus assuming quasi-responsibility.

Proper handling of the customer complaints pays off. In the three years prior to this book's publication, *INVEST* processed over 800,000 transactions and received just 808 customer complaints, or .1 percent. Of these, all but 25 were dealt with through a further explanation or some other immediate action. Of the 25 that went to arbitration, 18 were dismissed and the remaining seven, or just over .002 percent of the total of all transactions, were found for claimants. On these, any damages or costs were borne strictly by

INVEST under its subscriber agreement with no cost, damage, or publicity for the subscribing bank.

With such a small number of actual problems, the compliance procedure might seem like an excessive expense for which bankers rarely see a return. In some ways, compliance is like an automotive air bag; we hope it is never needed, but it's reassuring to know it's there.

Strategic Compliance

In-house compliance has become more respected in recent years as the banking industry has seen the wisdom in policing itself and cleaning up its act so regulators don't have to. Today, good compliance officers take part in senior management on a day-in, day-out basis, helping steer the firm. The department works best when reporting directly to the president of the company.

How can senior bankers make compliance work for their institutions? Attitude is everything—the regulators are there, they are not going away, work with them. From the very top down, compliance must be accepted and understood as an integral part of the team. Whether it is a $50-million rural thrift or a money center bank, compliance touches—without exception—every division, department, and person within the business—what is said as well as what is written. It is also compliance's job to find a way if a way can be found. If compliance tells someone "no," then the compliance officer's next words should be,

"But I believe we can do it this way, and still be in compliance."

It simply does not pay to skirt or violate any regulations, no matter how trivial they may seem. In recent years, some of the biggest firms in the insurance and securities business have come under fire for what may seem to some to be technical violations. They have risked their business reputations and incurred massive fines. These violations have cost the firms two essential and priceless ingredients: reputation and integrity.

Disclosure

One of the hottest issues of the 1990s has been the requirement that customers sign a disclosure form before they buy mutual funds in a bank. Without exception all bank investment clients should acknowledge that they know with whom they are transacting business and the nature of the products they are buying. Disclosure forms should clearly say things like:

- ☑ I understand what I'm buying is not guaranteed by the Federal government.
- ☑ I understand what I'm buying is not issued by this banking institution.
- ☑ I understand the value of this investment can and will fluctuate in value.
- ☑ I understand the interest rate can and will fluctuate.
- ☑ I understand loss of principal invested is possible.

☑ I understand I'm paying a commission.
☑ I've been given a prospectus."

These safeguards are intended to make it eminently clear to the consumer this is not bank business as usual. Customers who sign the disclosure form understand what they are buying.

But more subtle and perhaps more important is to insure the representative verbally covers all the important points in the disclosure forms. The representative can't be casual because both the broker and the customer should sign the form. This is a deterrent to omitting critical information in the clients' understanding of what they are buying.

The disclosure form ought to be standard operating procedure because of the nature of investment product services compared with the traditional banking activities. Everything a customer ever did in a bank before was predictable, whether it was a certificate of deposit or a loan. The customer often assumes, because it is being done in the hallowed halls of the bank, it will be predictable, too.

One way to make sure the disclosure is complete is to do it twice. First, use a disclosure document which must be signed by the client; second, include on all new account forms an acknowledgment clause which must be initialed by the client, not unlike accepting or declining insurance on car rental contracts where the client initials what they want or don't want.

Separate and Distinct

How is "separate and distinct" accomplished? How do bankers make sure the risk of being in the investment products business for the bank is acceptable with no threat to safety and soundness? At its heart, "separate and distinct" relates to the different expectations found in a bank versus a brokerage house. A consumer who buys a mutual fund from a brokerage firm knows the product is risky. But a consumer who buys the same product at a bank, because most of its deposits are government-insured, may assume the product is just like every other account he has in the bank. The reality is, of course, it is not.

To make sure the bank consumer who has been encouraged in this sense of security over many years of predictable transactions understands the difference, some banks are virtually putting up flashing signs in the lobby which say, "Risk! Risk! Risk!" While this may seem farfetched, the concept is not: bankers should do everything they can to make sure their customers know that what they are getting into is not what they're accustomed to.

This can be accomplished by separating the functions so customers understand when they leave the teller line and walk across the lobby to the investment kiosk or desk, they are literally leaving a familiar, insured haven and entering risky territory. A different visual appearance will make it amply clear there has been a change of venue, operating procedures, and results. The most dramatic interpretation of separate and distinct is for the customer to walk up a flight of stairs from the bank lobby to an investment center. In doing so, customers are physically removed from the warmth, trustworthy bank lobby to just another office, and one of the key advantages of investment services in the bank is lost.

Before there were platform programs, the difference between banking and brokerage was clearer. Series 7 brokers sat in the lobby in distinctive looking areas and all they did was brokerage. With platform programs it becomes complicated because the customer service individual who just cashed a CD is now the same person talking about mutual funds. These people don't spin around in their chairs and come out wearing different clothes. They don't metamorphose. They are the same bank employees they were a second ago, and there's a risk the customer will be confused about the nature of the product being discussed.

A good rule of thumb is: If it makes the customer ask: "What is this area?" bankers have succeeded in creating a separate and distinct environment. Signage is the key. The office or location can be almost anywhere as long as it's not in a teller line or positioned next to a teller line. Bankers can make sure clients know mutual funds and other products are not FDIC-insured and at the same time use the disclosure form as a tool for educating clients. By taking a positive approach, liability and complaints will almost be unheard of.

Regulators believe if a customer actually leaves the lobby and goes to another place, there is an emotional transition and a transfer of financial responsibility. They want to create a mental image of walking through an imaginary wall from bank to brokerage. The regulators are protecting the customers from themselves. Bank customers are accustomed to predictability and guarantees, no matter where the investment center is located or how it looks. Our responsibility as brokers is to explain what they are buying can and will fluctuate in value and there are no guarantees.

Compliance Due Diligence

Bankers must assure themselves that their own compliance departments or any third-party vendors are competent. They should kick the tires, speak to people other than senior management of the vendor, ask how a particular compliance procedure is implemented, and ask to see performance and product due diligence reports. Make sure the firm is truly up to standard, because once the choice is made, it attaches to the bank's reputation.

Banks will continue to earn trust through good business practices, supervision, education, suitability, disclosures, acknowledgment, and prompt handling of all customer complaints. These areas are essential to the success of an investment program. There are few mysteries about them. These tried and true procedures, implemented correctly, will assure that compliance is a positive and productive part of the program.

CHAPTER 10

The Future of Investment Products and Banking

We have come a long way in this business since the early 1980s. Perhaps the most significant change is that bankers are no longer worried that fee income products will disintermediate funds from the bank. They are now far more concerned about customer disintermediation and are much more comfortable that investment products are an excellent way to stop it. In fact, about 80 percent of all money invested through banks in mutual funds and other investment products comes from outside the institution. The profit power of what were once considered "alternative" products—in customer retention and increased relationships—has brought them to the very core of the retail bank.

Banks of virtually any size can avail themselves of a complete range of financial services and products by forming a partnership with a strong third-party marketer. Success depends chiefly on choosing the right company and then implementing its program with commitment. Bankers in small institutions in particular remain somewhat apprehensive about allowing a third party to provide vital services for their customers. And well they should be, because they must choose a third party that has first and foremost demonstrated a sensitivity to the needs of the bank. The people the marketer places in a bank must be thoroughly educated about and attuned to the culture and ambiance of their host.

The best third-party marketers will be a partner of the bank in the truest sense of that word, assisting it in serving its customers from financial planning through asset management. How banks utilize their third-party relationship to approach consumers—existing as well as new customers—will have a major impact on their ability to retain and gain market share. Banks of all sizes need to work with a firm that understands the lifestyle approach to marketing. The marketer should know about spending and saving habits of people in the bank's trading area, along with their propensity to buy investment products as well as other banking services. It should know how these prospects will respond to direct mail campaigns, telemarketing, ATM and point-of-sale announcements, and other marketing efforts.

Refocusing on the Basics

The fundamental areas of concern for banks in the 1990s are identifying niche markets and customer needs, providing superior customer service, and controlling expenses. The investment products business provides solutions for banks in all of these areas, particularly when their delivery is linked to financial planning services that provide customers with a strategic direction.

This book has demonstrated in ample detail how a variety of investment products are addressing a dramatically increased need for financial services on the part of bank customers. The primary vehicle for this has been through mutual funds. At the end of 1993, banks had $215.5 billion in assets under management, with bank managed funds representing 10.7 percent of the entire mutual fund market. More significant was the fact that in 1993, assets at bank-managed funds grew 34 percent, compared with 24 percent for the fund industry as a whole. Banks in the later 1990s will account for well over half of all mutual funds sales in the United States.

As we have discussed, the surge of bank proprietary funds is likely to fall off as institutions find the profits they generate are not as high as anticipated, or for regulatory reasons. At a conference on mutual funds in early 1994 sponsored by the *American Banker*, Barry P. Barbash, director of the Securities and Exchange Commission's division of investment management, warned banks not to jump into mutual funds as a "panacea for falling revenues." He said banks would be faced with an increasing set of complex regulatory issues revolving around fund assets, brokerage and sales practices, and transactions between the funds and their advisors. As a result, we believe there will most likely be a movement toward more private label funds, where an institution has established a relationship with a fund manufacturer, which provides the seed money to establish a fund for a specific bank.

Other products of significance—fixed and variable annuities, life insurance, and estate planning for bank customers—are becoming major bank offerings and are likely to increase in importance in the years ahead.

Annuities

Annuities will grow as a major source of income for people who are nearing retirement age. In 1980, 17 percent of new insurance company premium dollars went into annuity products. By the year 2000, it is predicted the figure will be 80 percent. Variable annuities are about the only investment opportunity that can keep up with inflation and do so without immediate tax consequence. In the latter part of this century, banks will take part in a major shift to the variable annuity for funding their customers' retirements. The products are appealing because people can take out just enough to live on and still watch the annuity grow overall in the course of a year. Yields for variable annuities are generally one to one and a half percent higher than for CDs or money market accounts.

There are precious few investments that offer this potential, and banks will serve a growing niche market by increasing their focus on the variable annuity. In the coming years, banks and third-party companies need to educate customers on the value of this product. Because variable annuities have received so much media attention in recent years, they are now distributed through wirehouses, banks, life insurance companies, and credit unions. Ten years ago, few people had even heard of them, and even today most people don't understand exactly what they are—only that they offer a way to save on taxes. Banks, if they link annuities to an overall investment and deposit program, are the most logical source of distribution for this product. The surge to these products is phenomenal.

In addition to heavy competition, the other downside for the variable annuities business is that it is subject to regulation by each state, and the regulatory requirements can sometimes make it difficult for banks to offer the product. But, banks should be in the variable annuities business—they are profitable, with average gross commissions often 100 to 200 basis points higher when compared with mutual funds.

Life Insurance

Life insurance is another product with immense potential in banks. There are relatively few people who make their entire living selling life insurance anymore, and yet the product still has great value for consumers. Banks have a golden opportunity to get into the retail side of the life insurance business, but they must help create an awareness of this need and build staffs prepared to offer the products to meet it. A certain level of sophistication and maturity on the part of sales staffs is needed to be successful in the life insurance business. Their approach must be coupled with financial planning to demonstrate to consumers the need for life insurance.

Capital needs analysis is a critical part of any thorough financial plan. It shows the need for life insurance and demonstrates how customers can use low cost dollars to fund the liabilities that will be left in the event of their untimely death. Banks should focus on a few strong products—for example, term life insurance and variable universal life. Bankers will need to put pressure on life insurance companies to assure a flow of products designed to meet the customers' needs within the bank coupled with the unique bank delivery systems of today and tomorrow. Third-party marketers already are forming alliances with life insurance companies to bring appropriate variable universal life products to market. These efforts are being accompanied by simplified application procedures, streamlined underwriting, and faster medical evaluations and rating of contracts.

Estate Planning

Banks offering estate planning services are experiencing one of the highest fee income streams of any alternative product or service in their institutions. The average commissions associated with an estate plan are substantial when compared to any other transaction.

The best way for the bank to fund estate plans is through survivor life insurance policies which are set up for an individual life or are based upon the second-to-die in a joint life policy. Thus, the funding is created that enables the beneficiaries of an estate to pay some or all of the estate costs. This avoids the necessity to liquidate estates to pay taxes or other expenses, which has often ruined entire estates.

In addition to generating fees, the additional benefit for the bank in providing estate planning is the funds stand a good chance of remaining with the institution if the estate stays intact.

Banks with trust departments have long offered estate planning services for their wealthiest customers. Using a third-party marketer with skills in this area opens up a substantial new universe for a service with a significant customer benefit.

Service and Product Distribution

Delivering services with added value will be the way in which banks maintain market share in the future. Bankers should not assume their customers will use their institutions as an exclusive financial products retailer. Customers will have other relationships with companies competing to provide the same services. The firms which add the most value will flourish in the financial future. The market itself will squeeze out inefficiencies and demand on wholesalers will increase.

People will always pay a premium for expertise from firms such as third-party marketers, but the value of these companies to banks will most likely evolve over the coming years. To control expenses, banks will utilize third parties in new variations of the full-service programs presently offered, including unbundled programs. For example, some banks may want to take a more à la carte approach, buying specific services such as compliance exams, education, profit potential studies, lead generating programs and other marketing services, financial planning, and other "products" that are less expensive for banks to outsource than to do themselves.

As banks enter new arenas, management often is hard-pressed to stay on the cutting edge of all the specialized services needed to serve its clients. The solution for all but the largest institutions is to use third-party firms to handle areas in which they don't have the manpower or expertise to handle internally. Broker/dealer is an example of an area most banks will find more efficient to outsource than to do themselves. (Appendix B can help bankers cost out the infrastructure required to properly serve customers in a start-up broker/dealer.) By outsourcing specialized services, the bank can concentrate on core functions such as building and maintaining relationships.

Compliance is another area all but the biggest banks should turn over to a quality third-party provider.

Just as banks outsource back-office and other functions, they will increasingly look to third parties for brokerage activities, particularly financial planning.

Marketing departments in banks are also making greater use of outside partners to develop materials to meet investment products needs. In part this is because of compliance issues, but a more significant reason is the skill the marketers have in reaching investment prospects. Education to improve productivity is commonly outsourced, as are commission accounting and benefits.

Bankers who want to maintain control over the investment products business have numerous options available to them already for outsourcing specific functions. These opportunities are likely to grow in the future and will help institutions to control costs and maintain efficiency.

A Look at the Future

For those in our industry who think we've been through an exciting time for the past decade, we suggest that the best is yet to come. The pace of change is accelerating and so too the resulting opportunities!

There will be a further blurring of the roles of banks, third-party marketers, brokerages, mutual fund, and insurance companies. New strategic alliances are likely to become the norm between firms which never before worked together. Because the cost of delivery of services is so high, they will need to leverage each other's strengths to achieve economies of scale. At the point of sale, the trend may well be to a highly specialized investment team which can handle the myriad of client needs. The team will have a specialist for investments, insurance and retirement, estate plans, and retail banking needs. The expanding complexity and variety of products will make it difficult for any individual to have complete knowledge in all fields. And while the customers will have more pricing options than ever before, so too will representatives have the option of offering as much or as little service as they feel is necessary. Remember, the true value-added service of tomorrow will be quality advice.

Investment product marketing in banks tomorrow will reflect the needs of a society that has moved a long way down the information super highway. Much of what we do will be accomplished electronically. A generation that is completely comfortable with computers will insist on high tech solutions to their financial needs. While we may never have a completely paperless society, there will be a dramatic increase in the use of electronic communications for the evaluation and purchase of financial services.

The irony is that in order to move into the future, banks will need to focus on the basics of their business as they apply to investment products. The interactive technologies will be a new way of delivering old-fashioned value—conservative investments that meet needs such as stratospheric costs for college education of their children and a fast growing "retirement gap" that threatens their own future.

The tremendous migration in recent years toward packaged products and managed portfolios will continue, although there is likely to be a change in the way these products are priced. It is probable that front-loaded mutual funds as we know them today will be largely replaced by some form of level load pricing. Investors will pay lower fees up front, and will have 100 percent liquidity when they sell funds, but in between they will be willing to pay for the appropriate investment of that money through an asset management fee.

Mutual fund vendors and distributors—including banks and their third-party marketers—will share in asset management fees as opposed to front loads. As a result, relationships with customers will be much more asset management-based rather than transactional.

The benefit for consumers should be increased performance and yield, and over time more revenue for banks because as performance improves, customers will invest more. Success will have its own rewards. While some bankers and many third-party marketers are opposed to this concept today because it casts uncertainty on the present revenue stream, we believe they will eventually embrace it as it becomes the standard distribution methodology of the future.

The consequences for the industry will be tremendous in the years ahead. Banks with proprietary funds, those with direct relationships with fund vendors or packagers, and third-party marketers and their banking partners have been accustomed to cash flows from up-front commissions. Sales fees fund all operations of the marketers—from due diligence and compliance through marketing and sales—and these are fairly employee intensive businesses. If these funds disappear, there will quite possibly be a period of upheaval, with some firms reducing staffs and overhead, others abandoning the business altogether because they are too thinly capitalized, and still others merging with stronger organizations.

The business will emerge after a four- to seven-year transition period healthier than ever, because once the shift to income based on asset management is complete, revenue streams will increase steadily and be more predictable.

Because the cost of distribution is so high a good number of banks with proprietary funds will find alternatives to these services, such as private label funds from major manufacturers or heavier reliance on third-party marketers as partners. Pricing of products will become much easier to deal with.

Distribution of investment products will also change dramatically. We think it is inevitable that mutual funds will be delivered through interactive television and via on-line computer services, in addition to traditional distribution through the bank lobby. The generation now in its twenties, thirties, and forties has complete comfort in the use of computers and interactive devices.

Computer users will be able to call up a prospectus on-line that is simple and easy to use and understand. Orders will be placed with a minimum of fuss, possibly through verbal commands and voice recognition systems. There will be more remote financial centers in mall kiosks which allow people to "visit their money" at any hour of the day or night. Wherever there is a high concentration of people—airports, shopping centers, office buildings—banks will establish one-stop shopping facilities for financial services. Consumers will interact with their representative over fiber optic networks and instantly get a prospectus delivered and confirmation statements for transactions.

Banks need to try as much as they can to keep the human touch in all of this, particularly those in smaller communities where the personal element has always been a bit more important than in the larger cities. Also, rural areas do not generate enough traffic to make it feasible to jump into the deep end of the technology pool because the hardware itself will remain fairly expensive.

The users of these advanced services will be far younger than the typical investment product customer of today. These computer literate customers will be first-time investors with planning needs and savvy, and they will feel comfortable with technology driven aides. In fact, they may be more motivated to buy if they can see their goals displayed in interesting graphics and dramatic "what-if" scenarios.

For banks, a big issue will be training existing staff in the use of computers and other advanced technology. Those who are not comfortable with sophisticated hardware and software will not be able to make their customers comfortable. They must prepare, because already today it is possible to execute trades on-line from a client's home or office. In banks as well as other institutions, people are sometimes measured by how much paper they shuffle, but those days are quickly coming to an end.

We believe the regulators will also play a role in this technological revolution, and there will be much more of a common ground on issues such as disclosure, separate and distinct. Technology will demand terms and conditions be explained in very simple and clear terms, and thus customer awareness and knowledge will improve. By the time the young people of today are investing, they will be asking questions not yet even thought about and getting answers which are clear and easy to utilize.

But, even as technology offers an opportunity to distribute products faster and more efficiently, banks should never lose sight of their principal advantage in the investment products marketplace: the trust and confidence they enjoy. People will continue to believe in their banks in part because banks have never been let down by the Federal government, and this has provided an impenetrable shield for consumers. Everything bankers do in this business should be aimed at assuring customers they can rely on the bank to provide prudent, cautious, and sound investment advice and execution.

To prepare for the future, banks must look at their core operations today to assure that they are well positioned for the rapid changes ahead. This process should also include a thorough evaluation of their current and prospective third-party associates. Does the partner have sufficient depth of capital, management, operation skill, experience with innovative programs, and ideas to bring the bank forward? Does the third party provide full indemnification to the bank? A partner offering only the advantage of an immediate cash savings may not be the right one for the long term unless it has a full array of products and services and the ability to integrate them into the basic fiber of the bank.

The future for everyone in the business is exciting. What we can all be sure of is that the pace of change and growth will not slow down any time soon.

Appendixes

APPENDIX A

Glossary of Terms

"A" Shares

"A" Shares, also known as "front-end loads" or, more recently, "front fee pricing" allow clients to pay a one-time initial sales charge at the time of the purchase and pay lower ongoing distribution fees and expenses. (See *Load Funds*.)

Adjustable Rate

The term applies to bonds or other investments that do not pay a fixed interest rate. Instead, the interest rate varies according to market conditions. "Adjustable" rate, "floating" rate, "variable" rate and "fluctuating" rates are synonymous. Examples of adjustable-rate investments are Series EE savings bonds, bank money market accounts, income mutual funds, adjustable-rate mortgages, prime rate trusts, and variable annuities.

A-I-S

Proprietary, systematic approach to financial planning developed by *INVEST* Financial Corporation which develops a profile of each client indicating just how important Appreciation, Income and Safety are to his or her overall investment strategy. These features are considered carefully in light of the client's personal goals and financial expectations. The end product is a score which indicates the client's objectives and concerns.

Alternative Investment Products

Securities, insurance products, and other investments not traditionally offered by a bank, including mutual funds, annuities, unit investment trusts, stocks, and bonds.

Annuities

An annuity is a contract between an insurer and recipient (annuitant) whereby the insurer guarantees to pay a stream of payments to the recipient in exchange for premium payment(s). The return of principal paid through premium payments is guaranteed by the insurance company. Interest rate levels and duration guarantees for interest rate payments vary with each contract and insurer but they are also guaranteed. An annuity provides for tax-deferred accumulation of interest on initial, and subsequent premiums, if any. Taxes on the interest and capital gains are not paid until the interest is withdrawn. The accumulated money may be withdrawn as a lump sum or over varying lengths of time as monthly income.

Fixed annuities guarantee the safety of the premium deposits. They also guarantee the initial interest rate for a specified time period.

Variable annuities are insurance-based investment products, which like other forms of annuities allow for growth of invested premiums to be free from taxation until withdrawals are made from the contract. Unique to variable annuities are several forms of investment alternatives which vary in both their potential for reward and risk. Variable annuity choices are broad enough that an investor can employ either an aggressive or conservative approach, or a combination of both, while enjoying the benefits of tax-deferred growth. Guarantee of principal from loss upon death of the owner is covered by a death benefit provision.

Arbitration

An alternative to suing in court to settle disputes between brokers and their clients and between brokerage firms. Traditionally, predispute arbitration clauses in account agreements with brokers automatically assured that disputes would be arbitrated by objective third parties and precluded court cases. In 1989, the Securities and Exchange Commission (SEC) approved changes that required brokers to disclose clearly when such clauses exist, prohibited any restrictions on customers' rights to file arbitration claims, and imposed stricter qualifying standards for arbitrators.

"B" Shares

Also called "back-end loads" or "back fee plans," allow clients to put more of their initial investment to work right away. Instead of an initial sales charge, Class B shares incur a contingent deferred sales charge (CDSC) if shares are redeemed early. The CDSC is reduced each additional year the shares are held, so eventually it is eliminated entirely. The higher annual distribution fees and expenses of Class B shares will result in a lower distribution rate than Class A shares. After a specified time Class B shares will automatically convert to Class A shares and no longer will be subject to higher distribution and service fees.

Bond

A promissory note given by a government or corporation to an investor, involving a promise to pay interest and to repay the par or face amount (also known as the principal) at a certain date. Interest is usually paid every six months, and the par value or face amount is usually $1,000. The payment date may be a few months or many years in the future. After a bond is issued, it may be bought and sold many times.

Bond Rating

Method of evaluating the possibility of default by a bond issuer. Standard & Poor's, Moody's Investors Service, and Fitch's Investors Service analyze the financial strength of each bond's issuer, whether a corporation or a government body. Their ratings range from AAA (highly unlikely to default) to D (in default). Bonds rated B or below are not investment grade—in other words, institutions that invest other people's money may not under most state laws buy them.

Broker/Dealer

A company that is registered with the NASD and SEC to perform general securities brokerage services. Broker/dealers that provide brokerage services to financial institutions act as a conduit through which securities transactions with the financial institutions' customers are processed. Such arrangements provide financial institutions the ability to offer brokerage services to its customers without forming its own "broker/dealer" subsidiary. Also referred to as "broker", "B/D", "BD," and "third-party firm."

"C" Shares

Also known as "level load" or "level fee plans." "C" shares allow clients to put more of their initial investment to work right away. Some may be subject to a contingent deferred sales charge (CDSC) for only the first year. Shareholders will incur higher annual service fees and expenses for their entire holding period.

Clearing Broker

A company that performs clearing services for a broker/dealer. Such services include execution of brokers' orders, preparing and mailing of trade confirmations to brokers' customers, maintaining customers' accounts and preparing and mailing monthly or quarterly statements to customers, providing margin trading, providing trade reports to the broker/dealer, and providing such other services as agreed between the clearing broker and the broker/dealer.

Closed-End Fund

A certain type of investment company or mutual fund which pools the money of many investors and uses it to buy a diversified portfolio of stocks, bonds, or both. A closed-end investment company is one that sells a specific number of its shares in a single offering. These shares are then usually traded on a stock exchange. Investors who buy shares in the investment company are indirectly investing in all the securities owned by that company.

Commission

The fee paid to a broker for executing a trade based on the number of shares traded or the dollar amount of the trade.

Compliance Department

Professionals who are responsible for ensuring that any activity complies with the rules of the exchange and those of the Securities and Exchange Commission or other regulatory bodies.

"D" Shares

"D" Shares, also known as wrap fee accounts, allow the distributor to buy funds from the mutual fund company at cost then wrap them with a fee. (See *Wrap Fee Accounts*.)

Deferred Annuity

Annuity whose contract provides that payments to the annuitant be postponed until a number of periods have elapsed, for example, when the annuitant attains a certain age.

Disclosure Statement

Within a financial institution, this document should be signed by clients stating they understand the product they are buying is not insured by the FDIC, the value of the investment can and will fluctuate, they understand they will be charged a sales charge on securities, they have received and read the prospectus provided for their investment and they understand the risks associated with the product they are buying. Often the representative is also required to sign the same document stating the customer was provided with this information and told about the costs and risks associated with the product.

While not yet currently required for each transaction, many firms utilize disclosure forms to insure the clients understand what they are buying at the time of the purchase and to avoid future arbitration.

Disintermediation

The movement of funds from low-yielding accounts at traditional banking institutions to higher-yielding investments in the general market. Since banking deregulation, disintermediation is not the economic problem it once was.

Diversification

Spreading of risk by putting assets in several categories of investments—stocks, bonds, money market instruments, and precious metals, for instance, or several industries, or a mutual fund, with its broad range of stocks in one portfolio. Liquidity diversification involves the purchase of bonds whose maturities range from short- to medium- to long-term, thus helping to protect against sharp fluctuations in interest rates.

Exchange Privilege

Right of a shareholder to switch from one mutual fund to another within one fund family—often, at no additional charge. This enables investors to put their money in an aggressive growth-stock fund, for example, when they expect the market to turn up strongly, then switch to a money market fund when they anticipate a downturn.

Hybrid Program

This type of program combines the best features of a Platform Program and Standard Program by staffing with a combination of full-time Series 7 registered representatives and Series 6 platform professionals.

Life Cycle

A progression through a series of different age, financial, career, and personal interest stages.

Load Funds

A mutual fund that is sold for a sales charge (load) by a brokerage firm or other sales representative. Such funds may be stock, bond, or commodity funds, with conservative or aggressive objectives. The stated advantage of a load fund is that the salesperson will explain the fund to the customer and advise him or her when it is appropriate to sell the fund, as well as when to buy more shares. (See "A" Shares.)

Lump Sum Distribution

Single payment to a beneficiary covering the entire amount of an agreement. Participants in Individual Retirement Accounts, pension plans, profit-sharing, and executive stock option plans generally can opt for a lump sum distribution if the taxes are not too burdensome when they become eligible.

Management Fee

Charge against investor assets for managing the portfolio of an open- or closed-end mutual fund as well as for such services as shareholder relations or administration. The fee, as disclosed in the prospectus, is a fixed percentage of the fund's asset value, typically 1 percent or less per year.

Managed Program

A turnkey program where a third-party marketing firm handles all aspects of establishing and managing the investment centers in the bank's branches including registration, compliance, marketing, financial planning, and education. With this type of program, the representative and manager are on the payroll of the third-party marketing firm. This program is otherwise similar to the Standard Program option and is often used in states that restrict the sale of annuities and other insurance products by bank personnel.

MCIF

Marketing Customer Information File (MCIF), also called Customer Information File (CIF), is a database providing banks a snapshot of their total relationship with each customer for a specific period of time. This report combines all the accounts of the customer, thus showing the complete relationship between the bank and the customer. The MCIF is a great tool for developing cross-selling strategies.

Modular Financial Planning

A financial plan geared to one element of the clients financial needs such as college planning, retirement planning, or portfolio review.

Mutual Funds

Funds operated by an investment company that raise money from shareholders and invest it in stocks, bonds, options, commodities, or other money market securities. These funds offer investors the advantages of diversification and professional management. For these services they charge a management fee, typically 1 percent or less of assets per year.

Mutual funds may invest aggressively or conservatively. Investors should assess their own tolerance for risk before they decide which fund would be appropriate for them. In addition, the timing of buying or selling depends on the outlook for the economy, the state of the stock and bond markets, interest rates, and other factors.

Mutual Fund Families

A mutual fund sponsor or company usually offers a number of funds with different investment objectives within its family of funds. For example, a mutual fund family may include a money market fund, a government bond fund, a corporate bond fund, a blue chip stock fund and a more speculative stock fund. If an investor buys a fund in the family, he or she is allowed to exchange that fund for another in the same family, usually with no additional sales charge.

National Association of Securities Dealers, Inc. (NASD)

The principal association of over-the-counter (OTC) brokers and dealers that establishes legal and ethical standards of conduct for its members. NASD was established in 1939 to regulate the OTC market in much the same manner as organized exchanges monitor actions of their members.

Net Asset Value (NAV)

The market value of each share of a mutual fund. This figure is derived by taking a fund's total assets (securities, cash and receivables) deducting liabilities and then dividing that total by the number of shares outstanding.

No-Load Funds

Mutual fund offered by an open-end investment company that imposes no sales charge (load) on its shareholders. Investors buy shares in no-load funds directly from the fund companies, rather than through a broker, as is done in load funds. Because no broker is used, no advice is given on when to buy or sell.

Open-End Fund

A mutual fund is considered "open-end" if it regularly sells an unlimited number of shares directly to shareholders and buys them back at NAV whenever shareholders wish to redeem or sell them.

Packaged Products

Specific types of products underwritten and packaged by manufacturing companies which can be bought and sold directly through those companies. Packaged products are not required to go through a clearing process. Packaged products include mutual funds, unit investment trusts (UIT), limited partnership interests, and annuities.

Platform Program

A program in which branch employees are licensed, typically with a Series 6 registration, to sell annuities and other insurance products, mutual funds, and unit investment trusts provided by a variety of companies selected for their suitability for bank clients.

Portfolio

Combined holdings of more than one stock, bond, commodity, real estate investment, cash equivalent, or other asset by an individual or institutional investor. The purpose of a portfolio is to reduce risk by diversification.

Product Vendor

A firm, such as an insurance or mutual fund company, which manufactures securities or insurance products, maintains selling agreements with third-party firms for the distribution of those products to subscribers, and provides marketing support materials. Most third-party marketing firms offer products which are manufactured by product vendors.

Proprietary Fund

A mutual fund or fund family which is manufactured by the bank, third-party firm, or company with which it is affiliated.

Registered Representative

An employee of a stock brokerage firm who acts as an agent to buy or sell stocks or bonds traded on the stock exchanges or the over-the-counter market. Registered representatives may also sell shares of open-end mutual funds, unit investment trusts and other investments. (See *Series 7* and *Series 6*.)

Securities and Exchange Commission (SEC)

The federal agency that administers U.S. securities laws. The SEC, headed by five appointed members, was created under the Securities Exchange Act of 1934.

Series 6

This registration qualifies a candidate for the solicitation, purchase and sale of mutual funds, variable annuities and variable life insurance contracts issued by an insurance company.

Series 7

An examination required of potential registered representatives, intended to test the candidates' basic understanding of the securities industry. The test, developed by the New York Stock Exchange and administered by the National Association of Securities Dealers, Inc., qualifies a person to sell every kind of security except commodities. Qualification includes the solicitation, purchase and sale of corporate securities, municipal securities, options, direct participation programs, investment company products, and variable contracts. Also called the General Securities Registered Representative Examination.

Simplified Employee Pension—Individual Retirement Account SEP-IRA

Pension plan in which both the employee and the employer contribute to an Individual Retirement Account (IRA). Under the Tax Reform Act of 1986, employees (except those participating in SEPs of state or local governments) may elect to have employer contributions made to the SEP or paid to the employee in cash as with cash or deferred arrangements (401(k) plans). Elective contributions, which are excludable from earnings for income tax purposes but includable for employment tax (FICA and FUTA) purposes, are limited to $7,000, while employer contributions may not exceed $30,000. SEPs are limited to small employers (25 or fewer employees) and at least 50 percent of employees must participate. Special provisions concern the integration of SEP contributions and Social Security benefits and limit tax deferrals for highly compensated individuals.

Securities Investor Protection Corporation (SIPC)

A government-sponsored organization created in 1970 to insure investor accounts at brokerage firms in the event of the brokerage firm's insolvency and liquidation. The maximum insurance of $500,000, including a maximum of $100,000 in cash assets per account, covers customer losses due to brokerage house insolvencies, not customer losses caused by security price fluctuations. SIPC coverage is similar in concept to Federal Deposit Insurance Corporation coverage of customer accounts at commercial banks.

Standard Program

A third-party marketing firm handles all aspects of establishing the investment centers in the bank's branches including registration, compliance, and education. Registered representatives and managers are dual employees of the third-party marketing firm and the bank. Compensation is paid by the bank.

Subscriber

A subscribing financial institution enters into an agreement with a third-party securities or marketing firm. Some firms refer to subscribers as "correspondents," "affiliates," "customers," or "clients."

Systematic Withdrawal Plan

A program in which shareholders receive payments from their mutual fund investments at regular intervals. Typically, these payments are drawn first from the fund's dividends and capital gains distribution, if any, and then from principal as needed.

Third-Party Marketer

A securities broker/dealer or marketing firm that provides brokerage and/or insurance programs to financial institutions on a third-party basis.

12b-1 Mutual Fund

Mutual fund that assesses shareholders for some of its promotion expenses. These funds are usually no-load, so no brokers are involved in the sale to the public. Instead, the funds normally rely on advertising and public relations to build their assets. The charge usually amounts to about 1 percent or less of a fund's assets. A 12b-1 fund must be specifically registered as such with the Securities and Exchange Commission, and the fact that such charges are levied must be disclosed. (See *No-Load Funds*.)

Transfer Agent

The organization employed to prepare and maintain shareholder account records.

Unit Investment Trust (UIT)

Investment vehicle, registered with the Securities and Exchange Commission under the Investment Company Act of 1940, that purchases a fixed portfolio of income-producing securities, such as corporate, municipal, or government bonds, mortgage-backed securities, or preferred stock. Unit holders receive an undivided interest in both the principal and the income portion of the portfolio in proportion to the amount of capital they invest. The portfolio of securities remains fixed until all the securities mature and unit holders have recovered their principal.

Wrap Fee Accounts

An account offering investors an assessment of their investment goals and risk tolerance, professional money management, payment of all fees and commissions, and monitoring of their portfolio and manager's performance. For this service, wrap accounts typically charge a fee of 1 1/2 percent to 3 percent of assets annually.

Wirehouse

National or international brokerage firm whose branch offices are linked by a communications system that permits the rapid dissemination of prices, information and research relating to financial markets and individual securities. Although smaller retail and regional brokers currently have access to similar data, the designation of a firm as a wirehouse dates back to the time when only the largest organizations had access to high-speed communications. Therefore, wirehouse still is used to refer to the biggest brokerage houses.

APPENDIX B

A Third-Party Marketing Audit

Reduction of expenses, regulatory pressures, increasing profits, building long-term relationships and maintaining a high level of customer service are top priorities in the banking industry. Third-party marketers which offer brokerage services and products to banks are, in theory, positioned to provide comprehensive and proven resources for supporting banks, their sales personnel, and most importantly, their customers. This audit provides a checklist of the resources required to run a successful financial services program in today's environment. Use it to review a current program or a third-party marketing company being considered for a new program.

	Existing Program	Program Under Consideration
Program Type		
Managed	_____	_____
Standard	_____	_____
Platform	_____	_____
Direct Product	_____	_____
Custom Product	_____	_____
Contract Flexibility		
1, 2, 3 Year Options	_____	_____
Production Bonuses	_____	_____
No Set-Up Fees	_____	_____
Customer Protection	_____	_____
Indemnification	_____	_____
Compliance		
Branch Exams	_____	_____
Surveillance	_____	_____
Regulatory Liaison	_____	_____
Reg. Rep. Registration	_____	_____
B/D Registration	_____	_____
Insurance Agent Licensing & Appointments	_____	_____
Risk Management	_____	_____
Operations		
Customer Service Guarantee	_____	_____
Program Support	_____	_____
Fixed-Income Desk	_____	_____
New Accounts Processing	_____	_____
Vendor Accounts Reconciliation	_____	_____
General Operations	_____	_____
Customer Service Desk	_____	_____

	Existing Program	Program Under Consideration
Sales		
Regional Account Managers	_____	_____
Regional Insurance Specialists	_____	_____
Field Training Directors	_____	_____
Telemarketing Assistants	_____	_____
Implementation Managers	_____	_____
Marketing		
Direct Mail Prospecting	_____	_____
Branch Revenue Forecasts	_____	_____
Branch Demographic Data	_____	_____
Advertising	_____	_____
Tri-Annual Marketing Kits	_____	_____
Monthly Publications	_____	_____
Local Public Relations Support	_____	_____
Education & Productivity		
Initial Rep. Training	_____	_____
Continuing Rep. Training	_____	_____
Platform Program Training	_____	_____
Banker On-Site Training	_____	_____
Public Seminars	_____	_____
Conference Services	_____	_____
Financial Services		
Financial Planning	_____	_____
Pension Services	_____	_____
Annuity/Insurance Services	_____	_____
Mutual Fund Services	_____	_____

	Existing Program	Program Under Consideration
Financial Services		
Research	_____	_____
Product Due Diligence	_____	_____
Monthly Investment Bulletins	_____	_____
On-Site Laptop Computer Financial Planning	_____	_____
Finance & Administration		
Commissions/Accounting	_____	_____
Human Resources	_____	_____
Technical Services	_____	_____
Facilities	_____	_____
Purchasing	_____	_____
Tax Preparation	_____	_____
General Accounting	_____	_____
Systems	_____	_____
Electronic Data Processing (EDP)	_____	_____
Proprietary Quote, Order Entry & Account Inquiry System	_____	
Products		
Fixed Annuities	_____	_____
Variable Annuities	_____	_____
Life Insurance	_____	_____
Mutual Funds	_____	_____
Unit Investment Trusts	_____	_____
Securities (Stocks, Bonds, etc.)	_____	_____

NOTE: Make sure the third-party marketing company has the necessary resources by visiting its headquarters and reviewing each specific support area.

About the Authors

Merlin R. Gackle
President and Chief Operating Officer

Merlin R. Gackle is President and Chief Operating Officer of *INVEST* Financial Corporation. Mr. Gackle joined *INVEST* in January 1990 as Executive Vice President and Director of Sales and has been involved in the day-to-day operations of the company including new business development, operations, implementation, customer service, national sales desk, and advanced technology.

He has nearly 23 years of experience in the brokerage and insurance industry, of which 18 years has been in management. Mr. Gackle's experience includes an extensive background in corporate financial planning, employee benefits, insurance distribution, and brokerage management.

Prior to joining *INVEST*, Mr. Gackle was senior vice president and national sales manager for Colonial Investment Services, Inc., of Boston, MA, where he was responsible for the sales and marketing of annuity products and mutual funds through a nationwide network with Colonial Investment Services, Incorporated.

Mr. Gackle is a dynamic speaker and has spoken at national conferences for banking and brokerage trade groups including the Bank Securities Association, Savings and Community Bankers Association, and Strategic Research Institute. He is a frequent commentator on the financial industry in the print and electronic media and has authored articles which have appeared in various industry publications.

Mr. Gackle holds a bachelor's degree from Eastern Montana College and completed graduate work at Portland State University. In addition, he was adjunct faculty at the University of Miami for the College of Financial Planning of Denver.

Donald F. Eller
Chairman and Chief Executive Officer

Donald F. Eller, CFA, is Chairman and Chief Executive Officer of *INVEST* Financial Corporation. Mr. Eller has over 31 years of experience in the investment industry and was appointed Chairman and Chief Executive Officer of *INVEST* in January 1994. Previously, he served as Senior Executive Vice President and Director of Client Services for Kemper Securities, Inc., one of the nation's largest full-service investment brokerage firms. In that capacity, Mr. Eller was responsible for the entire retail system of more than 150 branch offices and 1,500 investment consultants, as well as the products and services which support that system.

A veteran of the investment industry since 1962, he joined Prescott, Ball & Turben in 1986 as Director of Research and subsequently also became Manager of Institutional Sales and Trading. He has worked as an analyst with Merrill Lynch, as a portfolio manager with Investors Diversified Services, as a research manager for Abraham/Lehman Brothers, and in money management and administration at Roulston & Co.

Mr. Eller received his bachelor's degree in commerce and finance from Wilkes University in Wilkes Barre, PA, where he was named Outstanding Graduate. He received his M.B.A. from Fairleigh Dickenson University in New Jersey. He also participated in the Securities Industry Association's Institute at The Wharton School, University of Pennsylvania. Mr. Eller is a Chartered Financial Analyst having originally earned his designation in 1966. He has since qualified for recertification every year since it became possible to do so. Mr. Eller is also a member of the Association of Investment Management and Research, an international association which sets standards for research and ethical behavior.

Joel R. Kesner
Executive Vice President
Director of Sales

Joel R. Kesner is the Executive Vice President, Director of Sales for *INVEST* Financial Corporation. Mr. Kesner joined *INVEST* in April 1991 as Senior Vice President and Director of Financial Services and has 23 years experience in the financial industry.

Mr. Kesner is responsible for all aspects of sales at *INVEST* including maintaining relationships with existing subscribers, supervision of managed program activities, coordination with all product managers, development of economic and market themes to be utilized in the field, and overseeing the Vice President Regional Managers, Regional Sales Managers of Insurance and all *INVEST* Managers and Representatives. He also serves as the Director of Insurance.

Prior to joining *INVEST*, Mr. Kesner was First Vice President and Division Sales Director for Florida at Shearson Lehman Brothers, Inc. During his seven-year tenure, the Florida division was first in sales six times in both insurance and mutual funds. Mr. Kesner was also Vice President, Regional Sales Director, and Senior Financial Planner for Shearson in the Coral Gables office.

Mr. Kesner holds the designation of Chartered Life Underwriter, Chartered Financial Consultant, and has a Masters of Science in Financial Services.

Louis H. Newtson
Executive Vice President, Chief Financial Officer
Director of Finance and Administration

Louis H. Newtson is Executive Vice President, Chief Financial Officer and Director of Finance and Administration for *INVEST* Financial Corporation. Mr. Newtson joined *INVEST* in September 1989 as Chief Financial Officer and Senior Vice President. He was named Director of Finance and Administration and joined the Executive Committee in July 1990 and was named Executive Vice President in December 1993. Mr. Newtson has 26 years of experience as a financial officer in the securities industry. He is a member of the Board of Directors of *INVEST* Financial Corporation Holding Company, the parent of *INVEST* Financial Corporation.

Mr. Newtson is responsible for all corporate functions of Commissions, General Accounting, Taxes, Human Resources, EDP, Technical Services, and Facilities departments. In addition, the Director of Compliance and Director of Operations report to him.

Prior to joining *INVEST*, Mr. Newtson was Senior Vice President and Treasurer, Chief Financial Officer and a member of the Board of Directors at R. Rowland & Co., Executive Vice President and Treasurer, Chief Financial Officer and a member of the Board of Directors at Rowland, Simon & Co., and Vice President and Treasurer with Stifel, Nicolaus & Co., Inc. in St. Louis, MO.

He received a Bachelor of Arts degree from Beloit College and a Masters in Business Administration from Wayne State University.

Robert K. Burke
Senior Vice President
Director of Education, Telesales, and
Conference Services

Robert K. Burke is the Senior Vice President and Director of Education, Telesales and Conference Services of *INVEST* Financial Corporation. Mr. Burke joined *INVEST* in August 1991, bringing with him 14 years of experience in the financial industry.

Mr. Burke is responsible for all education programs and the ongoing development of new methods of instruction to increase the productivity of participants in the sales process. Under his direction *INVEST* has increased sales by 62 percent due to the *INVEST* Pro Plus System, a proprietary sales enhancement program. Mr. Burke is also responsible for *INVEST*'s three telephone sales groups and the firm's conference services department.

Previous to *INVEST*, Mr. Burke was the National Director of Sales and Marketing of Kemper Capital Markets. He also spent four years as the Manager of the Unit Investment Trust Department at A.G. Edwards & Sons, Inc. There he was responsible for all underwriting, trading, distribution, and administration of that packaged product. In addition, Mr. Burke was an associate in the Strategic Financial Planning and Analysis Group of Morgan Stanley & Company.

He obtained his M.B.A. in Finance from The Wharton School of the University of Pennsylvania.

Mary Ann Goodrum
Senior Vice President
Director of Implementation and
Product Management

Mary Ann Goodrum is Senior Vice President and Director of Implementation and Product Management at *INVEST* Financial Corporation. Ms. Goodrum's responsibilities include directing the efforts of the implementation managers responsible for introducing *INVEST* to all new banks in the *INVEST* network. In addition, Ms. Goodrum guides *INVEST*'s Product Management Department in its marketing relationships with product vendors, due diligence efforts, development of product recommendations, and performance tracking.

In her three years as Senior Implementation Manager, Ms. Goodrum was responsible for the conversion and introduction of one of *INVEST*'s largest platform programs at West One Bank. In addition, she implemented *INVEST*'s standard, managed and other platform programs into regional and community banks. Her implementation responsibilities encompass recruiting representatives, operations setup, introductions to bank employees and customers, and conversions from other broker/dealers.

Ms. Goodrum joined *INVEST* in 1986 and her prior responsibilities included vendor relations, new product introduction, new business development, strategic planning and financial analysis. Ms. Goodrum earned her M.B.A. in Finance at Vanderbilt University.

Ellen P. McCorkle
Senior Vice President
Director of Operations

Ellen P. McCorkle is Senior Vice President and Director of Operations at *INVEST* Financial Corporation. Ms. McCorkle joined *INVEST* in September 1991. With over 21 years experience in brokerage operations, she is responsible for General Operations, Customer Service, Program Support, and

Fixed Income. While at *INVEST*, Ms. McCorkle has been responsible for formulating customized analyses that evaluate staffing, workflow, policy and procedures, equipment needs, and appropriate service levels for *INVEST*'s Subscribers' Operations/Service Centers.

Prior to joining *INVEST*, she was with Shearson Lehman Brothers for 10 years and served as First Vice President - Divisional Operations Officer. In that capacity, she was responsible for operations, compliance, human resources, and financial administration for the South Central Division overseeing 50 offices with 750 Representatives and 450 Operations/Sales Support personnel. Previously, she was Operations/Administrative Manager for several major investment firms including Paine Webber, E.F. Hutton, and Thomson McKinnon.

John R. Richter
Senior Vice President
Director of Marketing

John R. Richter is Senior Vice President and Director of Marketing for *INVEST* Financial Corporation. As Director of Marketing, Mr. Richter is responsible for the retail marketing support provided to *INVEST* Centers in 45 states, as well as all communications and media/trade association relations supporting *INVEST*'s new business development efforts. Mr. Richter also oversees *INVEST*'s Marketing Technology Group, which provides revenue forecasts for existing and potential subscribing bank branches and comprehensive lead management programs.

Mr. Richter has 23 years of experience in sales and marketing and held positions in the banking, investment and retail industries. Prior to joining *INVEST*, he served as President and Chief Operating Officer of WestMark, a third-party marketing company based in Portland, OR, where he was responsible for operations, business development and marketing. Prior to WestMark, he served as Executive Vice President and Director of Marketing of Bankers First Corporation while also serving as President and Chief Executive Officer of its financial marketing services subsidiary, Lafayette Marketing.

Mr. Richter was with Sears in Chicago for 15 years and served as the National Sales Promotion Manager for one of the merchandising groups. Mr. Richter developed strategic merchandising plans on how to maximize sales potential with over 36 million credit card customers and 50 retail groups across the country.

Lynn M. Smelt
Senior Vice President
Director of Financial Services

Lynn M. Smelt is the Senior Vice President and Director of Financial Services for *INVEST* Financial Corporation. Ms. Smelt joined *INVEST* in March 1987 and has 11 years experience in financial planning administration.

Ms. Smelt's responsibilities include developing and administering *INVEST*'s financial planning support program and pension services. She is a

Chartered Financial Consultant, Chartered Life Underwriter, and a member of the International Association of Financial Planners and American Society of CLUs and ChFCs. Ms. Smelt earned her Bachelor of Arts degree in Marketing from the University of South Florida.

Prior to joining *INVEST*, Ms. Smelt was a Regional Marketing Associate for First Financial Planner Services, a subsidiary of Travelers, which provided financial planning firms with hardware and software support, regulatory assistance, product information, and training. Ms. Smelt also spent several years in the insurance industry focusing on estate and employee benefit planning.

Jeffrey W. Thornton
Senior Vice President
Director of New Business Development

Jeffrey W. Thornton is Senior Vice President and Director of New Business Development of *INVEST* Financial Corporation. Mr. Thornton joined *INVEST* in 1990 as Senior Vice President and Director of Sales for *INVEST*'s Western Division, bringing with him 10 years of experience in the financial industry.

Mr. Thornton has spent the last 13 years of his career exclusively marketing securities and investment-oriented insurance products through financial institutions. He has established sales operations within two of the largest money center banks within the United States where annual sales will total in excess of $1.5 billion. Moreover, Mr. Thornton has also contributed to the development and management of sales operations within four of the top 10 largest savings and loans within the United States, where there are now over 200 retail account executives generating over $1 billion a year in total sales.

Mr. Thornton's focus in establishing new sales organizations within financial institutions is to integrate cultures with a strong emphasis on cross training, proven recruiting methods, and strong sales management procedures.

Theodore T. Wdowiak
Senior Vice President
Director of Compliance

Theodore T. Wdowiak is Senior Vice President, Director of Compliance for *INVEST* Financial Corporation. Mr. Wdowiak was Director of Compliance with *INVEST* from 1982 through 1985 and rejoined the firm in June 1992. He has over 25 years experience in the securities industry.

Mr. Wdowiak is responsible for *INVEST*'s relationships with all securities, insurance and banking regulatory bodies which pertain to compliance with their rules and regulations. He is also responsible for the development and implementation of all compliance policies and procedures for the *INVEST* network.

Mr. Wdowiak began his career with the National Association of Securities Dealers, Inc. (NASD) and has also served as Director of Internal Audit at Merrill Lynch and Senior Vice President of Compliance and Audit at the Coffee, Sugar and Cocoa Exchange.

Mr. Wdowiak holds six NASD licenses including General Securities Principal, Options Principal, and Securities Sales Supervisor. Mr. Wdowiak earned his Bachelor of Science degree in Finance from New York University and attended Brooklyn Law School.

Bob Andelman
Co-author

Bob Andelman's work appears regularly in newspapers and magazines across the United States and Canada. He is also the Central Florida correspondent for *Business Week* and *Newsweek*, and a five-time Florida Magazine Association award winner for investigative reporting.

Mr. Andelman is also the author of *Stadium for Rent: Tampa Bay's Quest for Major League Baseball* (McFarland & Company) and *Why Men Watch Football* (Acadian House).

Allan Priaulx
Resource Media, Inc.
Project Editor

Allan Priaulx is President of Resource Media, Inc., a consulting firm in New York City which emphasizes the development and practical implementation of corporate strategies for financial services and media companies. Previously, Mr. Priaulx was Publisher of *American Banker*, the leading newspaper serving the banking industry, Vice President and Editorial Director of CNR Partners, and Vice President and General Manager of The Hearst Corporation syndication division, King Features. Mr. Priaulx began his career with United Press International, serving as a reporter, bureau manager and bureau chief in Paris with responsibility for news gathering in France and North Africa.

He is co-author of *The Almost Revolution* (Dell, 1969, with Sanford J. Unger) and has been a contributor to various magazines and books. He also has been a public speaker on media and banking topics.

Index

A
A shares, 173
Account(s)
  see Annuity, Cash,
    Certificate, Checking,
    Deposit, Fixed, Money,
    Passbook, Savings
  fees, see Annual, Investment
  forms, 151
  management, 23
  records, 146
  set-up fees, 111
Accumulation, 66
Achievers, 66
Acquisition, 72
Active marketing, 47
Adjustable rate, 173-174
Adjustable-rate mortgages, 174
Administration fees,
  see Annual, Loan
Administrative
  functions, 132
  skills, 87
Advanced sales class, 87
Adversity, 38-40, 50
Advertisements, 75
Advertising, 76
A-I-S, see Appreciation
Alternative investment(s), 2
  products, 6, 118, 174
  program, 29

Alternative products, 12, 116
Amendment fees, see Plan
Annual
  administration fees, 111
  investment account fees, 111
Annuity/annuities, 1, 24, 36,
  70, 73, 76, 111, 115, 158-159,
  174-175, 185
  see Deferred, Fixed, Variable
  accounts, 57
  licenses, 132
  sales, 33, 83, 140
  products, 51, 117, 158
  vendors, 45
Appendices, 171-197
Appreciation, Income, and
  Safety (A-I-S), 174
Arbitration, 23, 31-33, 38-39,
  175-176
Area growth projections, 64
Asset(s), 10, 12-14, 46, 66, 97,
  98, 107, 157
  see Cash, Customer, Fund,
    Retirement
  growth, 57
  management fees, 165
  value, 54
  see Net
ATM, see Automated
Audit, see Marketing,
  Third-party

213

Automated teller machine
    (ATM), 16, 70, 156

B
B shares, 176
Baby
  boom generation, 8
  boomer(s), 61, 102
    generation, 99
    market, 7
Back-office
  activities, 13
  departments, 30
  functions, 12, 163
Bank
  see Commercial,
    Community associates
    class, 88
    education programs, 90
  branches, 61, 112
  broker, 40
  brokerage
    operations, 60
    pensions marketing, 109-112
  broker/dealers, 31
  CDs, 111
  clients, 98
  customers, 89, 138, 154
  employees, 11, 138
  holding company, 17
  investment
    business, 140
    products, 85
    programs, 83
  management, 11, 40, 41, 100, 125
  managers, 34, 41, 90, 105
  marketer, 51, 61, 97
  marketing
    campaigns, 75
    departments, 76
    initiatives, 61
    plan, *see* Integrated
  personnel, 33, 100
  products, 89, 103, 118
  program, 39
  representatives, 75, 103, 107
  roles, 163
  senior management, 12
  subscribers, 29
Bank-based brokers, 91
Bankers, 1-16, 21, 24, 60, 62, 83, 84, 88, 97, 156
  see Community,
    Nonregistered, Senior
Banking
  see Electronic
  agencies, 140
  delivery system, *see* Retail
  education, 83-96
  environment,
    see Sales-oriented
  future, 155-169
  improvement, 17-42
  program, *see* Correspondent
Bank-wide financial planning
    campaign, 100
Basics, refocusing, 157-161
Bond(s), 1, 176, 183
  see Government, Growth,
    High-yield, International,
    Junk
  rating, 177
Bottom-up
  analysis, 137
  approach, 45
Branch
  level, 122-124

Index 215

managers, 105, 122, 123
personnel, 124, 125
staff, 123
Broker(s), 1-16, 39, 78, 91, 92, 106, 143, 144, 146, 151, 184
  see Bank, Bank-based, Clearing, Series, Third-party
  performance, 41
Brokerage(s), 17-42, 49, 86, 89, 144, 163
  see Bank, Community, Full-service
  activities, 142
  business, 5
  firms, 1, 2, 92, 127
    see Third-party
  house, 125, 152, 191
    insolvencies, 188
  operation, 10
    see Bank
  practices, 158
  representatives, 62, 122, 133
  service, 142, 177, 193
Brokerage in a box, 32-38
Broker/dealer, 5, 11, 12, 17, 19, 28-31, 38, 39, 42, 135, 140-143, 162, 177, 178
  see Bank, Independent, In-house, Securities, Third-party
  operation, 18
  services, 136
  subsidiary, 177
Buttonwood Agreement, 139-140
Buy-in, 79, 89
  see Management

C
C shares, 177-178
Cal Fed, 117-118
Calculation fees,
  see Distribution
Campaigns, 77-78
  see Bank-wide, Financial planning
  budget, 80
Capital, 32, 56
  gains, 175
  investment, 135
  needs analysis, 160
  ratios, 22
Cash assets, 134
Cash flow, 8, 9
Cash management accounts, 2
CD, see Certificate
CDSC, see Contingent
Certificates of deposit (CDs), 1, 5, 91, 101, 125, 153, 158
  see Bank
  accounts, 123
Certified Financial Planner (CFP), 27, 108
CFP, see Certified
Chartered Financial
  Analysts, 24
  Consultant (ChFC), 27
Chartered Life Underwriter (CLU), 27
Checking, 2, 5, 77
  accounts, 41, 60, 61
ChFC, see Chartered
CIF, see Customer
Class(es), 85-88
  see Advanced, Bank, Managers, Platform,

Productivity, Representative, Sales
Clearing, 12, 23, 131, 132, 142
  broker, 178
Client
  base, 27
  categories, 66
  needs, 164
  relationships, 27
Closed-end
  fund, 189
  mutual fund, 182
CLU, *see* Chartered
Commercial banks, 129
Commission, 31, 178, 112, 119, 163
  see Gross, Up-front
    expectations, *see* Pro forma
  products, 25
Commitment, 119-122
Commodities, 183
Communication compliance, 147-149
Community bank(s), 4, 12, 14
  brokerage, 129-138
  network, 13
Community bankers, 130, 138
Compensation, 38, 41-42, 121, 122
  see Incentive
  packages, 134
Compliance, 12, 23, 23, 87, 130, 139-154, 162
  see Communication, In-house, Strategic
  department, 179
  due diligence, 154
  exams, 162
  examiners, 146

expenses, 36
officers, 149
  see Third-party
  personnel, 148
  requirements, 47
Compliance-approved
  letters, 73
  materials, 27
Computerized order entry
  systems, 28-29
Confirmation statements, 142, 167
Congress, 55, 141
Consumer protection, 142
Contingent deferred sales
  charge (CDSC), 176
Corporate
  goals, 79
  securities, 187
  staffing/support, 26
Correspondent
  banking program, 14
  programs, 134-136
Cost efficiency, 15
Credit, *see* Deposit/credit
Credit
  cards, 5, 60, 127
  unions, 159
Cross-leverage, 15
Cross-referral
  goals, 90
  ratios, 106
Cross-selling, 10
  opportunities, 68
  ratios, 76
CSR, *see* Customer
Cultural barrier, 88-89
Customer
  see Bank, Trust

Index

assets, 60
base, 130
data information, 13
defections, 57
definitions, 62-66
demographics, 62-66
disintermediation, 155
file system, 132
information, 69
   file (CIF), 182
   see Marketing
needs, 61, 89, 130
   identification, 65-66
relationship(s), 20, 21, 56
   leveraging, 73
   risk, 55
retention, 64, 126, 134
service, 4, 9, 14, 97, 157, 193
   focus, 9-11
   operations, 130
   representatives (CSRs), 88, 91, 115, 121, 124-126
statements, 142
transactions, 39
trust, 92, 97
   leveraging, 97-113

D

D shares, 179
Data companies, 69
Deferred annuity, 179
Delivery system, *see* Banking, Investment, Retail
Demographic(s), 64
   see Customer
   data, 68
   information, 66
Deposit
   see Direct, Insured, Payroll

accounts, 41
balances, 63
products, 128
Deposit/credit margins, 5
Deregulation, 180
Direct mail, 70, 71
   campaigns, 156
   fulfillment material, 74
   pieces, 76
   prospecting program, 74
Direct payroll deposits, 70
Disciplinary action, 144
Disclosure, 150-152
   documents, 146
   forms, 151, 153
   see Regulatory-tested
   policies, 123
   statement, 179-180
Disintermediation, 2, 4, 98, 133, 134, 180
   see Customer
Distinct, *see* Separate
Distribution
   see Lump, Pension
   calculation fees, 111
   center, 61
   fees, 111, 173
   methodology, 165
   network, 46
   outlet, 135
   strategy, 20
Diversification, 24, 47, 110-111, 180, 183, 185
   see Portfolio
Dividend yields, 44
Document fees, *see* Plan
Drive-through windows, 70
Due diligence, 19, 24, 43-57, 130

see Compliance, Product
expenses, 36
guidelines, 55
process, 29

E
Earnings
  see Price/earnings
  growth potential, 45
  growth rates, 44
Economies, *see* Short-term
Economy/economies of scale, 15, 32, 132, 162
Education, 12, 13, 23, 26, 84-88, 162, 163
  see Bank, Banking, Team
  efforts, 123
  importance, 124-128
Educational program, *see* Third-party
Efficiency, 31-32
  see Cost
Electronic banking, 70
Employee(s)
  see Bank, Non-registered, Retail
  cost, *see* Fixed
  pension, *see* Simplified
Employment tax, 187
Enhanced fee income, 136
Equity
  lending, *see* Home
  market, 44
  offerings, 47
ERISA, 110
Estate
  plan(s), 164
  planning, 160-161
Ethnic mix breakdown, 64

Exchange privilege, 180
Execution, 23
Expense(s), 31-32
  see Compliance, Due, Fixed, Legal, Up-front
  budgets, 25
  costs, 54
  ratio, 54
Experience, 22-23

F
FDIC, *see* Federal
FDIC-insured products, 153
Federal Deposit Insurance Corporation (FDIC), 55, 140, 142, 153, 179, 188
Fee(s), 20, 111, 165
  see Account, Amendment, Annual, Asset, Document, Distribution, Enhanced, Investment, Loan, Management, Plan, Processing, Service, Termination, Trustee
  break points, *see* Sales
  income, 3, 12, 13, 19, 36, 63, 88, 117, 119, 125-126, 128
  program, 123
  stream, 160
FICA, 187
Field staffing/support, 26
Filters, 44, 85
Financial advisory services, 8
Financial capacity, 47
Financial plan(s), 41, 90
Financial planners, 124
Financial planning, 8, 9, 12, 13, 27-28, 36, 37, 61, 76, 90, 95, 97-113, 130

Index 219

see Modular
campaign, *see* Bank-wide
capabilities, 13
clients, 98
firms, 127
organizations, 86
process, 105
services, 7, 23, 99, 109
system, 33
Financial products, 61, 70
retailer, 161
Financial sectors, 45
Financial services, 2, 3, 9, 61, 157
see Personal
Financial strength, 21-22
Fixed
accounts, 51
annuity, 51
employee costs, 61
expenses, 36
Fixed-income
lines, 47
market, 44
401K plans, 15, 112, 187
Front-loaded mutual funds, 165
Full-service
brokerage, 13
programs, 162
Fund(s)
see Closed-end, Growth-stock, Load, Manufactured, Mutual, No-load, Open-end, Private, Proprietary, 12b-1
assets, 158
manager, 54, 55
manufacturers, 20, 55, 158
packagers, 165

source, 41
vendors, 165
FUTA, 187
Futures, 51

G
General Securities Registered Representative Examination, 187
Glossary, 173-191
Goal(s), 78, 84, 94, 122
see Corporate, Cross-referral, Sales
setting, 64
Government
bonds, 47
spending, 44
Gross
commissions, 33, 35, 118, 132, 159
national product, 44
Growth
see Asset, Tax-deferred
bonds, 47
projections, *see* Area
rate, *see* Earnings
Growth-stock fund, 180

H
Hesitation, 105-107
High-risk
investments, 83
securities, 83
High-yield bonds, 51
Home equity
lending, 5
loans, 61
Hybrid program, 37-38, 181

I

Implementation, 24, 136-138
Incentive(s), 88, 121, 126
  see Monetary, Nonmonetary
  compensation, 122
  payments, 116
  programs, 25, 81
    see Performance
Income, 6-7, 60
  see Fee, Fixed-income,
    Median, Personal,
    Retirement
  mutual funds, 173-174
  offerings, 47
  potential, 57, 122
Indemnification, 21, 32, 38,
  142, 169
Indemnity, 136
Independent broker/dealer, 32
Individual
  Retirement Account (IRA),
    181
    see Simplified
  securities, 111
Inflation, 1, 158
Information, 66-70
  see Customer, Demographic,
    Marketing, Needs-based,
    Need-to-know
  conversion, 70-72
  generating action, 68
  services, 28-29
Infrastructure, 29, 162
  see In-house
In-house
  broker/dealer, 12, 19, 30
  compliance, 149
  infrastructure, 6
Insulation, 39-40

factor, 33
Insurance, 111, 151, 164
  see Life
  agencies, 140
  business, 150
  companies, 1, 52, 97, 127, 163
  organizations, 86
  products, 33, 50, 57, 117, 185
  vendors, 130
Insured deposits, 83, 123
Intangibles, 130
Integrated bank marketing
  plan, 68
Integration, 116
  process, 123
Interest rate, 1, 2, 5, 44, 103,
  150, 173, 180
  marketplace, 54
Internal Revenue Service
  (IRS), 110
  filings, 111
International bonds, 47
INVEST University, 95-96
Investment(s), 77, 87, 164
  see Capital, High-risk,
    Marketing, Mutual fund
  account fees, Annual
  behavior, 65
  business, 95
  companies, 98
  Company Act of 1940, 190
  decisions, 55
  flexibility, 110
  portfolios, 24, 108
  product(s), 3, 7, 18, 20, 21,
    25, 35, 36, 41, 57, 60, 90, 103,
    124, 128, 129, 135, 155, 166
  see Alternative, Bank,
    Packaged

business, 101, 125
delivery system, 85
executive, 34
future, 155-169
industry, 22
representatives, 15, 105
program, 18-19, 31, 38, 120, 133
  see Bank
  integration, 115-128
  manager, 13
  philosophy, 91
representatives, 84, 86, 90, 100
services, 2, 3, 130
  program, 100
transaction, see Needs-based
trust, see Unit
IRA, see Individual

J
Junk bonds, 52

L
Legal expenses, 36
Lending, 5
  see Equity, Home
Leverage/Leveraging, 110
  see Customer
Liability/liabilities, 12, 18, 38
Licensed personnel, 25, 26
Life cycle, 6, 62, 65, 89, 103, 181
  see Personal
Life insurance, 9, 115, 159-160, 161
  products, evaluation, 50-52
  sales, 83
Limited partnerships, 185

Liquidity, 165
Lists, see Clean, Private, Profiled
Litigation, 30
Load funds, 181
  see No-load
Loan(s), 41, 60, 77, 99
  see Home, Mortgage
  administration fees, 111
Long-term needs, 106
Lump sum distribution, 181

M
Managed program, 33-34, 182
Management
  see Time
  buy-in, achievement, 79-81
  fee, 53, 55, 56, 182, 183
  see Asset
Manager(s)
  see Bank, Branch, Fund, Investment, Money, Portfolio, Program, Sales, Third-party
  class, 87
Manufactured funds, 56
Margins, 36
  see Deposit/credit, Profit
Market
  index, 72
  profile, 65
  segmentation systems, 66
  share, 19, 127
Marketers, see Bank, Third-party
Marketing, 12, 13, 23, 130, 131
  see Active, Bank, Pensions, Telemarketing
  audit, see Third-party

Customer Information File
 (MCIF), 59, 68, 182
 costs, 54
 departments, 163
 details, 64-65
 efforts, 156
 expenses, 18
 initiatives, *see* Bank
 investment, 135
 materials, 111
 partner, 29
 plan, 79
 programs, 11, 15, 36, 78
 proven techniques, 75-78
 secrets, 59-81
 skill, 6
 solution, 80
 support, 26-27, 47
 technology, 33, 63, 73
Marketing-based incentive
 programs, 4
Matrix, 68
MCIF, *see* Marketing
Median household income, 64
Merger, 72
Modular
 financial planning, 183
 planning, 103-104
Monetary
 incentive, 25
 policy, 44
Money
 manager, 56
  see Third-party
 market accounts, 2, 158, 173
 market securities, 183
Mortgage(s), 51, 99
 see Adjustable-rate
 loan, 129
 application, 91, 92, 127
Mortgage-backed securities,
 190
Motivation, 122-124
Motivational campaigns, 19
Mutual fund(s), 1, 3, 21, 36,
 70, 73, 76, 115, 126, 150, 157,
 163, 174, 180, 183, 185
 see Closed-end, Front-
  loaded, Income, Open-end
 business, 118
 company, 179
 distributors, 165
 families, 183-184
 investments, 189
 manufacturer, 13, 30
 product selection, 46-50
 programs, 110
 sales, 83, 140
 sector, 46
 vendors, 45, 130, 165

N

National Association of
 Securities Dealers (NASD),
 18, 23, 31, 141-145, 148, 162,
 177, 184, 187
Needs
 see Client, Long-term, Retail
 analysis, *see* Capital
Needs-based
 information, 62
 investment transactions, 88
 relationships, 85
 selling, 89
Need-to-know information,
 28, 70
Net asset value (NAV), 184

Index

New York Stock Exchange, 140, 141, 187
No-load funds, 184
Nonlicensed personnel, 25, 26
Nonmonetary incentives, 25
Nonregistered
  bankers, 90
  employees, 143
North American Securities Administrators Association (NASAA), 143

O

OCC, 55, 142
Office of Thrift Supervision (OTS), 55, 142
Open-end
  fund, 184-185
  mutual fund, 182, 186
Operational costs, 61
Order entry, 142
  systems, *see* Computerized
Order tickets, 146
OTC, *see* Over-the-counter
OTS, *see* Office
Outsourcing, 162, 163
Overhead costs, 129
Over-the-counter (OTC), 184
  market, 184, 186

P

Pacific Stock Exchange, 141
Packaged
  investment products, 91
  products, 30, 40, 111, 185
Partners, *see* Third-party
Partnerships, 5, 156
  see Limited
Passbook accounts, 1

Payroll deposits, *see* Direct
Pension(s), 15
  marketing, *see* Bank brokerage
  package, 110
  plan distribution, 109
  services, 95, 109, 111
  training, 111
Performance, 10, 26, 48, 52, 55, 71
  see Broker
  expectations, 41-42
  control, 29
  incentive program, 123
  reviews, 42, 87, 116, 122
  criteria, 121
  risk, 53
Personal
  consumption, 44
  financial services, 27
  income, 44
  life cycle, 59
  risk, 55
Plan administration, 111
  services, 110
Plan amendment fees, 111
Plan document fees, 111
Planning services,
    see Retirement
Platform
  people, *see* Series
  personnel, 35, 41, 117
  program, 35-37, 118, 181, 185
  representatives class, 86
  staff, 125
Point-of-sale
  announcements, 156
  brochures, 26
  materials, 62, 76, 78

pieces, 75
set up, 64
Portfolio, 47, 51, 185
  see Investment
  analysis, 27
  diversification, 111
  managers, 45
  review, 183
  turnover, 50
Preferred vendor(s), 24, 47
  list, 52
Premium, 161, 175
Price/earnings
  multiples, 45
  ratio, 44
Prime earners, 66
Principal, 54
Private label
  fund, 56, 158
  option, 56
Private lists, 71-72
Pro forma, 13
  analysis, 25
  commission expectations, 133
  revenue projection, 137
Pro Plus, 92-95
Processing fees, 111
Product
  see Life insurance
  categories, 95
  depth, 24
  differentiation, 48
  distribution, 161-163
  due diligence, 23
  evaluation, 53
  industries, 49
  mix, 13
  needs, 64
  selection, 12, 43-45

  see Mutual fund
  vendor, 185-186
Productivity, 17, 35, 87, 163
  see Representative, Sales
  class, *see* Sales
  tasks, 133
Professional touch, 107
Profiled lists, 71
Profit
  control, 29
  margins, 39
  potential, 63-64
    studies, 162
  sharing, 112
Profitability, 17
  see Program
  projections, 132
Program
  manager, 87
  profitability, 31
Promissory note, 176
Promotion, 79
Proprietary fund(s), 166
  route, 53-56
Prospecting programs, 72-75
Purchasing propensity, 64

Q

Qualitative/Quantitative
  input, 45
Quality spreads, 45

R

Real estate holdings, 51
Recordkeeping, 131, 146
Referral, 88, 95, 126
  generation, 100
  machine, 84
    development, 89-91

Index

network, 80
programs, 76
system, 91
Registered
  representative, 36, 142-144, 186, 188
    see Series, Third-party
    Examination, see General
  sales representatives, 132
  Securities Principal, 144
Regulator(s), 144-146, 168
  see Securities
Regulatory
  approval, 30
  environment, 18
  hurdles, 29
  issues, 43
Regulatory-tested disclosure forms, 143
Reluctance, 105-107
Representative(s)
  see Bank, Brokerage, Customer, Investment, Platform, Registered, Sales, Series 6, Series 7, Third-party
  class, 85-86
  productivity, 93
    see Sales
  satisfaction, 96
Request for proposal (RFP), 29
Retail
  account, 112
  bank activities, 116
  banking
    delivery system, 85
    needs, 164
  employee, 121
  services, 143
Retention rates, 20

Retired, 66
Retirement, 8, 164
  assets, 102
  income, 108
  gap, 164
  plan(s), 110
  planning, 183
  services, 27
  programs, 101
Returns, 48
Revenue(s), 3, 13, 34, 35, 64, 136
  forecasting, 64
  projection, see Pro forma
  streams, 166
  volume, 17
  yield, 6
Reward, 175
RFP, see Request
Risk, 10, 19, 30, 32, 175, 179
  see Customer, High-risk, Performance, Personal
  reduction, 185
  spreading, 180
  tolerance, 89, 183

S

Sales
  see Structured
  agreement, 46, 47
  assistants, 13, 87
  charge, 173
    see Contingent
  class, see Advanced
  culture, 119
  fee break points, 145
  goals, 4, 63
  interview, 89, 95
  managers, 120

materials, 76
motivation, 4
orientation, 76
personnel, training/
supervision, 143
practices, 158
programs, 34, 35, 116, 117
representative(s), 32, 34
  see Customer, Registered
productivity, 92
staff, 97
support productivity class, 87
system, 92-95
Sales-oriented banking environment, 106
Savings accounts, 1
SEC, see Securities and Exchange
Sector spreads, 45
Securities
  see Corporate, High-risk, Individual, Money, Mortgage-backed, Third-party
  agencies, 140
  broker/dealer, 189
  business, 150
  principals, 146
  regulators, 147
  transactions, 177
Securities Act of 1933, 140
Securities and Exchange Commission (SEC), 18, 31, 141-145, 157, 175, 177, 179, 186, 189
Securities Investor Protection Corporation (SIPC), 188
Securities-related transaction, 32
Seed money, 158

Self-policing, 144
  system, 145
Self-regulation, 140-144
Senior bankers, 149
Senior executives, 105, 119
Senior management, 11, 28, 33, 79, 105, 116, 117, 122, 149, 154
  see Bank
SEP, see Simplified
Separate and distinct, 142, 152-154
Series 6, 132, 186
  platform people, 37
  registered professionals, 124
  registration, 36, 185
  representatives, 86, 87, 118
Series 7, 132, 187
  broker, 37
  registered representative, 37
  representatives, 87, 117
Service
  distribution, 161-163
  fees, 178
Set-up fees, see Account
Short-term economies, 30
Signage, 153
Simplified Employee Pension (SEP), 112, 187-188
  Individual Retirement Account (SEP-IRA), 187-188
SIPC, see Securities Investor
Site selection, 64
Social Security, 102
Spiff, 36
Staffing, 12, 64
Standard(s)
  program, 34-35, 181, 182, 188
  setting, 19-29

Index

Start-up costs, 30
Sticker shock, 101
Stocks, 1
Strategic compliance, 149-150
Structured sales program, 33
Subscriber, 188-189
Success, 79
  factors, 14-16
Support
  programs, 130
  services, 111
Systematic withdrawal plan, 189

T

Talent pool, 91-92
Tax, *see* Employment
Tax incentives, 44
Tax Reform Act of 1986, 187
Tax-deferred growth, 175
Tax-free
  offerings, 47
  relationships, 45
Team education, 79-81
Telemarketing, 156
Tellers, 88, 91, 115, 121, 125
Termination fees, 111
Third-party
  associates, 168
  basis, 189
  broker, 2
  broker/dealer, 2, 32, 127
  companies, 159
  compliance officer, 147
  educational program, 11
  firms, 6, 24, 27, 28, 31, 84, 111, 126, 137, 146, 162
    control maintenance, 11-14
  manager, 38

marketer, 6, 11-12, 14, 17, 32, 33, 39, 40, 46, 48, 51, 57, 66, 69, 130, 131, 136, 137, 141-145, 147-148, 156, 161, 163, 165, 166, 189, 193
marketing, 38, 96, 188
  audit, 193-197
  brokerage firm, 111
  company, 132, 193
  firm, 10, 14, 21, 25, 31, 35, 70, 109, 110, 182, 187, 188-189
  money manager, 55
  partners, 37
  provider, 53, 162
  registered representative, 38
  securities, 188
Time management, 87
Timing, 1-4
Top-down approach, 44
Training, 12, 23, 84-88, 121
Training/supervision, *see* Sales
Transaction(s), 152
  execution, 142
Transaction-only
  clients, 98
  relationship, 98
Transfer agent, 189
Trust, 107-109
  see Investment, Unit
  customers, 99, 109
  departments, 7, 161
  services, 98, 99
Trustee fees, 109
Turnover, 49
  see Portfolio
12-b1 mutual fund, 189

U
UIT, *see* Unit
Underwriting, 160
Unit investment trust (UIT), 1, 111, 174, 185, 186, 190
  sales, 83
Up-front
  commissions, 165
  expenses, 30

V
Value, 45, 150
  see Asset, Net
  statement, 90
Value-added
  approach, 3
  services, 14, 15, 21, 85, 131, 135, 164
Variable annuities, 51, 158, 159, 174, 186
Vendor
  see Annuity, Fund, Insurance, Mutual fund, Preferred, Product
  agreements, 22
  valuation, 53
Volatility, 49

W
Walk-in traffic, 91
Wholesales prices, 111
Wirehouses, 91, 97, 159
Withdrawal(s), 111
  plan, *see* Systematic
Wrap fee accounts, 190-191

Y
Yield(s), 134, 158
  see Dividend, Revenue
  curve, 45